Miniature Embroidered
PATCHWORK
Projects in 1/12 Scale

First published 2003 by
Guild of Master Craftsman Publications Ltd,
166 High Street, Lewes, East Sussex, BN7 1XU

Text and designs copyright © Margaret Major
Copyright in the Work © Guild of Master Craftsman Publications Ltd

ISBN 1 86108 341 6

A catalogue record of this book is available from the British Library.

Publisher: Paul Richardson
Art Director: Ian Smith
Production Manager: Stuart Poole
Managing Editor: Gerrie Purcell
Commissioning Editor: April McCroskie
Editor: Dominique Page
Designer: Rob Wheele, Wheelhouse Design
Photographer: Christine Richardson
Illustrator: John Yates
Typeface: Berkeley

Colour origination by Icon Reproduction
Printed and bound by Stamford Press Pte Ltd (Singapore)

A note about measurements

Measurements are in imperial, with approximate metric equivalents
in brackets. Please note, however, that metric conversions may
have been rounded up or down to the nearest equivalent.
Only one set of measurements should be used, either imperial
or metric, and the two must not be mixed.

A note about the charts

Thread colour codes refer to the threads used in the projects. The
colours in the charts and the keys that accompany the charts are for
reference only.

Miniature Embroidered
PATCHWORK
PROJECTS IN 1/12 SCALE

Margaret Major

GUILD OF MASTER CRAFTSMAN PUBLICATIONS LTD

To my late mother, who encouraged my love of all things creative, and to my husband Peter, daughter Elizabeth, son-in-law Simon (my computer guru), son Andrew and daughter-in-law Amanda for their generous and enthusiastic support during the writing of this book.

Foreword

I first met Margaret Major at a dolls' house fair where her rainbow patchwork quilts really caught my eye. On closer inspection I realized that it wasn't tiny patterned squares pieced together, but finely sewn embroidery stitches creating the design. I hadn't seen anything like this in miniature before. The work was beautiful and it was difficult to believe that the quilts really had been hand-stitched. But there was Margaret demonstrating how it was done and making the process look so easy.

Luckily, I also had the chance to talk to Margaret at her home and view her own dolls' house and other stitching projects. She is as charming a woman as you could hope to meet. She is so enthusiastic about her craft and having spent time improving her skills on a course, is now eager to pass on that knowledge to others.

There is no doubt that miniature crafts, such as embroidery, bring a dolls' house to life. You may choose to have a finished quilt ready on your bed, but you could also have one half-completed on a miniature frame with a sewing basket nearby. It will appear to anyone viewing the dolls' house that the miniature occupant has just stepped out for a moment.

Margaret's book offers you a means of personalizing your dolls' house by using her unique designs and bringing your own miniature home to life.

Christiane Berridge
Editor, *The Dolls' House Magazine*

Contents

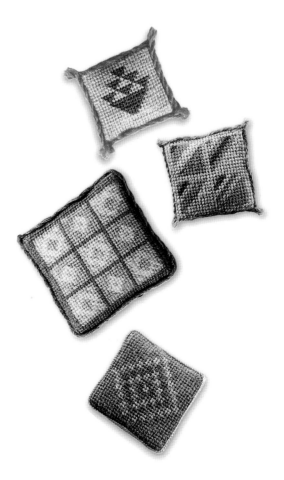

Bedcover exhibited at Levens Hall, Cumbria, England: the earliest
known example of English patchwork, circa 1708

Introduction

Patchwork, the term given to joining small pieces of fabric together, often in a pattern, to form a larger piece of fabric, has been practised for over 2000 years, but it was the North American settlers that devised most of the patterns still used today. The earliest known example of English patchwork, believed to date from about 1708, can be seen at Levens Hall in Cumbria, England (see facing page). This bedcover and other bedroom furnishings exhibited there are unique in the history of English patchwork. It is presumed the second wife of Colonel Sir James Grahme (who owned the house at the time) worked them with her stepdaughters and other members of the household. The octagonal and cruciform patches contain quite large uncut motifs from the prints, so they present an interesting record of the Indian textiles imported into the country at the end of the seventeenth century.

Over the last 250 years the popularity of patchwork has flourished, making it an ideal addition to many dolls' houses. But anyone who has tried producing 1/12 scale patchwork, handling pieces of material a mere ¼in (6mm) across, will know just how difficult it can be, and for many of us one attempt is enough! However, most of the popular patchwork patterns we see today comprise triangles, squares, diamonds and rectangles, all of which adapt extremely well to counted-thread embroidery.

In compiling this book I have been careful to include designs that will appeal to needleworkers at all levels of expertise, from projects using simple one-patch designs, through to the more complex patterns for those who like a bit of a challenge. All of the designs have the distinct advantage that they require very little counting of fabric threads, as the patterns are made up of small shapes, just as they would be in pieced patchwork. But even if you have never done any needlepoint before, you will find all the information necessary to get you started, with advice on equipment and materials, basic stitches, techniques, and colour guidelines. I have also included chapters on adapting the projects, creating your own designs, plus many tips I have found to be useful over the years, to help you achieve truly professional results.

To enable you to see at a glance which project would be best suited to your level of ability I have graded each of them as follows:

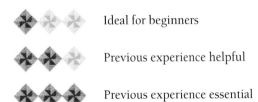

Ideal for beginners

Previous experience helpful

Previous experience essential

If you are unsure of your ability, I suggest you start with one of the simpler projects. You will find that all you need is a little practice to give you the confidence with which to try the more complex pieces.

I am sure that exploring the possibilities of 1/12 scale embroidered 'patchwork' will give you as many hours of enjoyment that piecing together treasured scraps of fabric continues to give many thousands of people all over the world today. And if you are new to counted-thread embroidery, I very much hope this book will lead you on to a relaxing and rewarding pastime.

Chapter 1

Getting Started

Materials and Equipment

Equipment

I have listed below the basic pieces of equipment required to complete the projects in this book. Of course, there are plenty of other non-essential items available on the market that are likely to tempt you, some of which I have also listed. Most embroiderers manage to gather a few of these 'non-essentials', as they can all add to the pleasure that this pastime provides.

Essential equipment

- Small, sharp-pointed scissors
- Range of blunt-ended tapestry needles, sizes 22–28
- Embroidery needles, size 10
- Quilting needles, size 10 for very fine work
- Wooden or card frames
- Selection of evenweave fabrics
- Variety of threads
- Magnifying aid, if your eyesight requires it
- Small lamp, preferably with a daylight bulb
- Drawing pins
- Fabric glue

Non-essential equipment

- Thread organizer
- Quick-stitch ripper
- Colour wheel
- Needle-threading aid

Frames

I am possibly a bit of a bore on the subject of frames! I always use one, and encourage every miniature needleworker I teach or meet to do the same. Obviously, you can work without a frame, but I can never think of any justification for doing so. When your fabric is mounted properly in a frame you have a

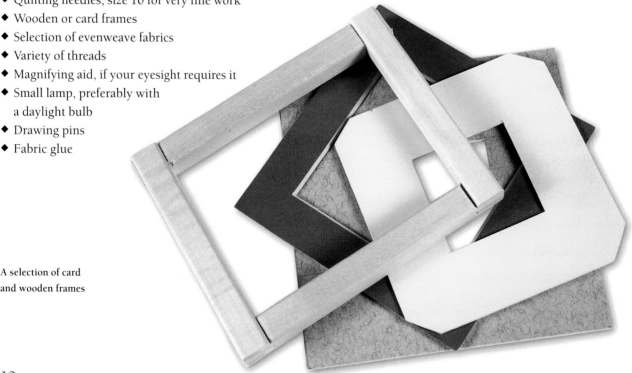

A selection of card and wooden frames

12

taut surface on which to build your stitches, the holes are easier to see, the fabric will distort less, and your stitches will be more evenly tensioned.

There are a variety of frames available on the market. Many people choose to use lap frames, as they enable both hands to be kept free, but slate frames are a popular alternative. Like most lap frames, they have a strip of webbing on two sides onto which you sew your fabric. Personally, I find them a little heavy and cumbersome for most miniature embroidery. I prefer to use small, square or rectangular frames, available in packs from needlework suppliers (names and addresses given on page 135). The different lengths of softwood slot together to produce the size and shape of frame you require. They can be used over and over again and take drawing pins easily. Alternatively, for very small, fine work, I use a handmade card frame. (For advice on how to make a card frame and how to frame your fabric, see Basic Stitches & Techniques, pages 18–19.)

Needles

For most of the projects in this book, I have used tapestry needles that vary in size from 22–28. They have blunt ends, so are less likely to split the threads of the stitches you have already worked. They also have a long eye, so are relatively easy to thread. However, very fine fabrics require finer needles. When working on 35tpi linen I use a size 10 embroidery needle, and on 40tpi silk gauze a size 10 quilting needle, which is short and very fine – not so easy to thread, but worth the effort for the effect it

gives! As a guide, your needle should hang in the fabric when inserted into a hole. If it falls through it is too small, and if it needs a push to get it through, it is too large.

Scissors

You really need two pairs of scissors for miniature embroidery: a large pair for cutting your pieces of fabric straight, and a small embroidery pair with sharp points to use as you work. An unpicking tool is useful, but not essential.

Magnifying aids

Many of the miniaturists I meet are, like me, no longer in their first flush of youth, and if you fall into this category and know your eyesight is not as good as it was, don't worry – there are plenty of magnifying aids on the market. Even youthful eyes may appreciate a little help with particularly fine work.

A variety of magnifiers are available: there are some that hang around your neck; floor-standing magnifiers that are combined with a light (very useful); and others that clamp onto a table. I use magnifying glasses, which I bought from my opticians. They are very convenient to take anywhere with my embroidery, and I find them easy to use; but it does mean that I need a separate lamp with a daylight bulb in the evenings. Good needlework and craft shops sell various magnifying aids, so it is worth investigating which is most suitable for you. Your time spent embroidering will be much more enjoyable if you can see your work without straining your eyes.

Materials

Fabrics

Evenweave fabrics, including cotton, linen, interlocked mono canvas and silk gauze have been used for all the projects in this book. The fabrics are mostly sold by the metre, or packaged in small pieces, except for silk gauze, which is usually sold by the inch at specialist needlecraft shops. Evenweave fabrics are distinguished by the number of threads per inch (tpi) or sometimes by the number of holes per inch (hpi). Therefore, if your fabric is 18tpi you will be able to count eighteen vertical threads along every inch of fabric. For 28tpi you will be able to count twenty-eight vertical threads, and so on. The lower the number of tpi the larger the holes, and the higher the tpi the smaller the holes. Obviously, the more threads there are to the inch, the more detail you will be able to work into your pattern, so it is a good idea to use as high a count as you are able to see (see Magnifying Aids, page 13).

For miniature embroidery, I prefer not to use a fabric with less than 18tpi, as the number of strands of thread you would need in your needle to cover the fabric would result in a bulky finish, which may appear out of scale. One of the objectives in 1/12 scale embroidery is to keep everything as fine as possible, so the finished pieces look appropriate in a dolls' house setting. The fabrics used in these projects range from 18tpi to 40tpi, but, if necessary, it is simple to alter the fabric to one that you can see better to work on. For example, the Roman Stripes cushion (see pages 38–39) has been worked on 25tpi linen with a stitch count of 26 x 26, giving a finished size of approximately 1in (25mm) square. If, however, you would prefer to work on 18tpi, your finished cushion would measure approximately 1½in (38mm) square. This is a perfectly acceptable size for a 1/12 scale cushion, but you must remember to use more strands of threads in your needle to cover the larger holes. In the case of 18tpi, you will need at least three strands. (For more advice on changing the fabric size, see Adapting Projects, pages 130–131.)

Evenweave fabrics

Threads

There are hundreds of beautiful embroidery threads available on the market, many of which are suitable for miniature embroidery. For most of the projects in this book I have used DMC stranded cotton (you will find a thread conversion chart at the back of the book on page 135). Occasionally, though, I have used a very fine silk.

Stranded cottons

Stranded cottons have a soft sheen and are ideal for miniature work. Many are 6ply, so they need separating before use. By doing this, you only use as many strands in your needle as required to cover the fabric. (For how to separate the strands, see Basic Stitches and Techniques, page 19.) You may like to mix two single strands of different colours in your needle at the same time for an alternative effect, as illustrated in the Random Patch rug design (see pages 61–63).

Silks

Silk threads are usually more expensive than stranded cotton, but in miniature embroidery we use relatively small amounts, so it is worth gradually building up a collection of them. Fine silks are often in single-strand skeins, and come in a wide range of colours and weights.

Choose the thickness according to your fabric. Personally, I would rather use one strand of a slightly thicker silk than two strands of fine.

Wools

I don't often use wool for my embroidery, but if I do I usually buy a fine-quality Medici. This produces a beautifully smooth result, which is not too 'furry'. It is most suited to carpets.

Synthetic threads

The colours of some synthetic threads are very tempting, but I find they are more difficult to work with in miniature embroidery: the tiny stitches don't seem to sit as comfortably as they do with natural fibres. Don't be afraid to experiment for yourself, though.

6ply stranded cottons

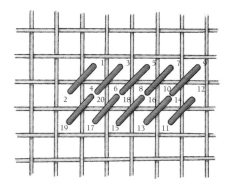

Tent stitch:
Stitches from
left to right

Tent stitch:
Stitches from
right to left

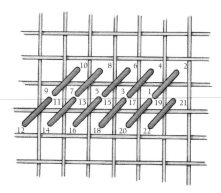

Basic Stitches
and Techniques

Stitches

Most of the projects in this book are worked in tent stitch, but for two of the designs I have used Rhodes stitch. If you prefer, in place of tent stitch, you could work in half-cross stitch, but I find the basic tent stitch provides a much neater result and a pleasing finish to the back. It also gives a firmer piece of embroidery, so it is particularly suitable for items such as rugs and wall hangings. However, tent stitch can distort the fabric, so it is essential not to pull the stitches too tightly. They should lie gently and evenly along the top of your fabric.

If you usually work in cross stitch or half-cross stitch you may need to practise the basic tent stitch before you start on your project. I suggest you use a spare piece of canvas that is easy to see, such as 18tpi, and work a few rows to familiarize yourself with how the stitch is formed.

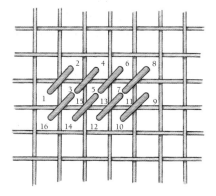

Half-cross stitch:
Stitches from left
to right

Half-cross stitch:
Stitches from
right to left

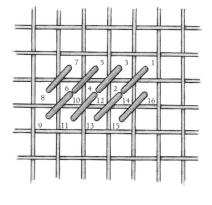

Rhodes stitch

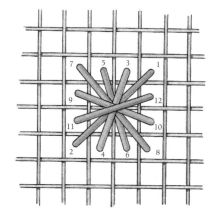

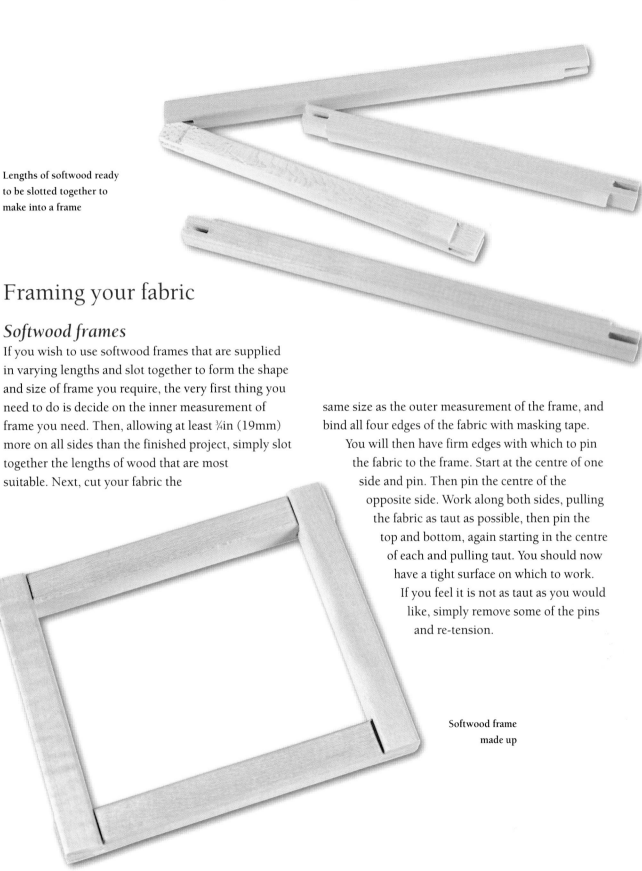

Lengths of softwood ready
to be slotted together to
make into a frame

Framing your fabric

Softwood frames

If you wish to use softwood frames that are supplied
in varying lengths and slot together to form the shape
and size of frame you require, the very first thing you
need to do is decide on the inner measurement of
frame you need. Then, allowing at least ¾in (19mm)
more on all sides than the finished project, simply slot
together the lengths of wood that are most
suitable. Next, cut your fabric the same size as the outer measurement of the frame, and
bind all four edges of the fabric with masking tape.

You will then have firm edges with which to pin
the fabric to the frame. Start at the centre of one
side and pin. Then pin the centre of the
opposite side. Work along both sides, pulling
the fabric as taut as possible, then pin the
top and bottom, again starting in the centre
of each and pulling taut. You should now
have a tight surface on which to work.
If you feel it is not as taut as you would
like, simply remove some of the pins
and re-tension.

Softwood frame
made up

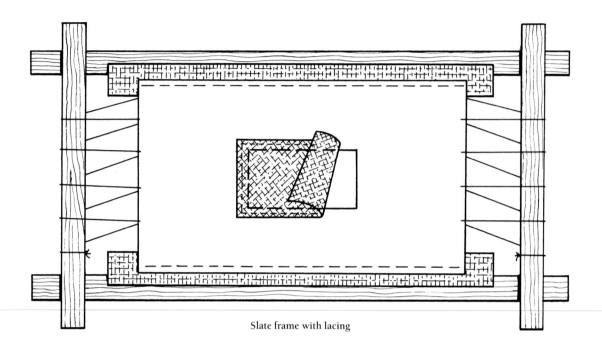

Slate frame with lacing

If you choose to use a lap frame or slate frame you will need to sew your embroidery fabric onto the centre of a larger piece of scrap material, then cut away carefully the scrap material behind the area you intend to stitch. You can then attach the material to your frame by sewing it to the strip

of webbing attached to the top and bottom sections of the frame (use backstitch and very strong thread). Roll both bars outwards until the material is nicely tensioned, then fix with wing nuts. Finally, you will need to lace the material to the sides of the frame, making stitches approximately 1in (25mm) apart.

Card mounts

Mounting your fabric on card is a gloriously simple thing to do, and works particularly well for small projects, such as cushions or stool tops, when using fabrics with a count of 35tpi or more. Card mounts have the additional advantages of being light to hold (reducing strain on your wrist) and easy to pop into a bag if you wish to take your embroidery out with you.

Card mounts

You will need some stiff card, a metal ruler and a sharp craft knife. The card should be approximately 4–5in (102–127mm) longer and wider than the finished size of your embroidery. With the ruler and craft knife, cut the centre carefully from the card, leaving an even width of border all around. Cut your embroidery fabric a little smaller than the overall measurements of your card mount, and, with masking tape, stick the top of your fabric to the top border of your mount. Pull the fabric as taut as possible, then stick the bottom of the fabric to the bottom border of the mount. Stick both sides in the same way, again ensuring the fabric is as taut as possible. Turn the mount over. Your fabric is now conveniently mounted and ready to work on. Card mounts can be used several times, as the masking tape is easily removed. I keep a selection of different-size mounts ready for use.

Preparing your thread

Most of the projects in this book have been stitched using DMC Stranded Cotton, which is six stranded and therefore needs separating for miniature embroidery. The easiest way to avoid tangles is to cut a length of about 12in (300mm) and hold it at the top, away from your lap. Pull one thread at a time, straight up, away from the rest, then let each one untwist thoroughly. If you are using two or three threads, lay them side-by-side after separating them and thread through your needle at the same time. By separating the threads in this way, you will remove the 'twist' and get a nice flat stitch. The projects in this book will either need one, two or three threads in your needle, and the number is shown at the start of each piece.

Starting and finishing your thread

I usually work with a length of thread that is no more than 12in (300mm), and for very fine work about 7in (178mm). Longer lengths begin to fray as they are pulled backwards and forwards through the fabric, giving the stitches a 'furry' appearance.

I would advise against leaving knots in your work. Instead, knot your thread and take the needle down from the front to the back about ½in (13mm) away from where you are going to start stitching, then work towards the knot. That way you will be working over the piece of thread at the back and securing it. When you reach the knot, snip it off carefully. Alternatively, if you are in the middle of working an area of the same colour as the thread in your needle, take the new thread carefully under about ½in (13mm) of the previous stitching, and then continue.

When a project requires two threads in your needle, the easiest way to start is to cut the thread double the normal length and to thread both ends through your needle at the same time. Bring your needle up from the back in the position you wish to start, but do not pull the loop right through. Instead, leave a small loop at the back of your work. Take the needle down from the front in the correct position and catch it in the loop. Finally, pull the thread until the stitch sits neatly on the front of your work. This method produces a neat back, and is economical with thread.

To finish a piece of thread you are working with, just run your needle under the back of the last few stitches of the same colour and snip close to your work.

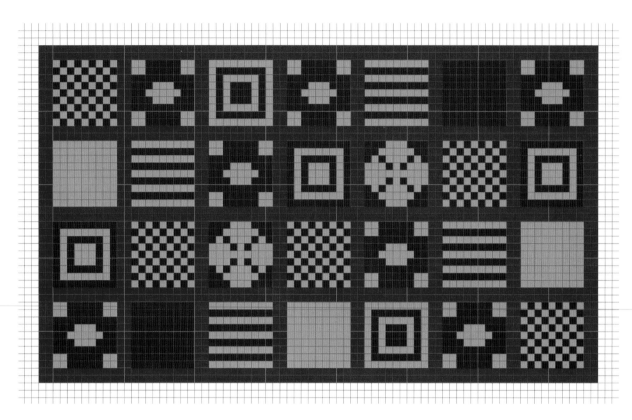

An example of a chart

Reading the charts

Each coloured square on the charts represents one stitch, and each stitch is worked over one thread of fabric. The lines on the charts do not represent the threads of your fabric, but are there merely to show the number of individual stitches. The colour of the square represents the colour of the thread required to work the stitch. It is that easy! So although a project with a detailed pattern looks more complicated, it is really only a question of changing the colour thread in your needle more often. It is a good idea to have several needles on the go at the same time, each with a different-colour thread. This saves a lot of re-threading when you need to change colour.

Where I have used random-dyed silks, and the colours graduate to form different colours along the length of the skein, the colours shown on the chart are a guide only to give you an indication of the overall shade of each of the colours I chose. For further explanation of this, please see the relevant project details.

I recommend working the patterned areas of the charts first, then working borders, if any, afterwards.

Mistakes

We all make them! Fortunately, it is possible to go over the odd stitch or two that you have worked in

the wrong colour. Just re-work the stitches in the correct colour over the top of the old ones, pulling the thread fairly tightly so that the stitches don't sit proud of the others.

If you spot a recent mistake, you may find you can pull the thread back carefully and undo the offending stitches one at a time. This is best done from the back of your work. If the mistake was made some way back, you will need to tackle it extremely carefully with a small pair of sharp-pointed scissors or an unpicking tool. Don't rush the process, as it is so easy to cut a thread or two of the fabric as well as the stitching, but should this happen there is no need to panic. I have found the problem can be rectified by applying a tiny amount of fabric glue carefully to the small area that is affected, on the back of your work, making sure you cover the damaged area. Allow it to dry thoroughly. The glue will fill in the holes around the damaged area, but your needle can easily be pushed through the glue to form new holes.

Blocking

Blocking is the term used to describe a method of returning your finished piece of embroidery to its correct shape. This is only necessary if it has become distorted during working, and with many of the small items in this book it is unlikely to be a problem. However, should you feel it necessary, this is how I go about it:

First of all, remove your embroidery from its frame. Place a piece of plain white paper, larger than your fabric, onto a wooden board. Then, using a ruler and pencil, draw on the paper the exact shape of the

original size of your fabric (not just the embroidered part), making sure the corners you draw are completely square. Cover this tightly with plastic food wrapping, which you can secure at the edges of the board with drawing pins or sticky tape. Next, spray your embroidery very lightly with clean water on the back, but be careful not to use so much water that you wet the fabric – only the threads should be damp. Turn the work face up and, using drawing pins, pin the fabric onto the board, lining it up exactly with your pencil-drawn shape. You will need to pull it to shape as you go. When you are satisfied, leave it to dry naturally for a day or so, then remove the pins. If the embroidery was very distorted, you may need to repeat the process once more.

NB: This method cannot be used if your threads are not colourfast. To test them, wash a few lengths of spare thread and pat dry on a piece of absorbent paper towelling. There should be no transfer of colour to the towelling. If the colour does transfer, you can still use the above method, but omit the water and leave your embroidery pinned to the board for at least a week.

Colour Guidelines

I always feel I am first attracted to an item by its colours, so I choose my colours carefully. Colour can completely alter the way a piece looks; for example, soft, pastel shades result in a gentle, sunny look, while dark colours used in a dolls' house evoke images of a wood-panelled study or dining room.

I always encourage people I teach to try their own colour combinations. After all, if you are embroidering a pattern designed by someone else, but use colours you have chosen, you will have an entirely unique piece of embroidery.

To consider how your chosen colours relate to one another, hold them together in natural light. Does one of them 'jump out at you' as being too bright or is one just too dull? Keep trying different colours until you find a combination that pleases you.

Remember, in miniature embroidery there has to be more definition between the colours than in full-size embroidery. When colours are too similar, they tend to fade into one another, giving an all over 'grey' appearance that can make it difficult to see the pattern.

You will find the colour wheel on this page very helpful if you intend to design your own patterns or alter the colours of the projects in this book. As a rough guide, colours taken from opposite sides of the colour wheel complement each other, a vibrant effect is achieved if you use three colours that are an equal distance apart, and a relaxing effect is achieved by using colours from just one third of the colour wheel. You may also find it useful to have some colour cards from paint manufacturers. These can be cut up and the colours arranged until you have an idea of what you like.

Before starting a new project, it is always worth embroidering small samples of the pattern in different colour combinations on a spare piece of embroidery fabric. This will give you a very clear idea of which you like best and how the finished piece will look.

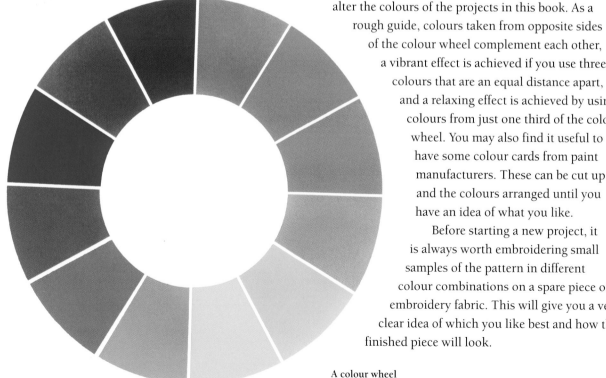

A colour wheel

If you like a co-ordinated look in your dolls' house, try altering the colours of any of the projects in this book to colours you have already used.

Lastly, take inspiration for colour combinations from furnishing fabrics, wallpapers, wrapping papers, etc. You will find that sometimes the most unlikely combinations look wonderful together. Keep a folder into which you can slip various pieces of paper or material that have caught your eye – you will find this an invaluable source of reference when you come to choose colours for a project.

A pattern worked in different colour combinations

Fabric samples can inspire your colour choices

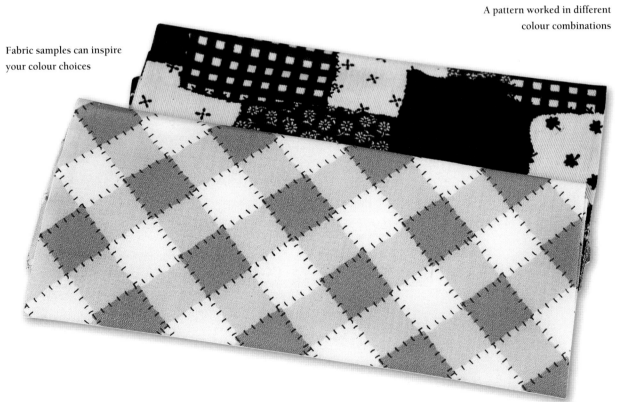

Chapter 2

Cushions

Cushions have been used in the home for centuries, designed originally to improve the comfort of plain, hard furniture. But since the popularity of embroidery in Victorian times, their use has grown to such an extent that there is now barely a room in most people's houses that does not contain at least one cushion. There can be no doubt that cushions add a decorative touch and a look of cosiness to all homes, including dolls' houses.

I have based the cushions in this book on original patchwork patterns, and you will see that a variety of effects can be achieved by using very simple designs. They are all quick and simple to embroider, making them ideal projects for a first attempt, or for when you want something that is not too taxing to work.

DIFFICULTY RATING

Single-Patch

You should find this cushion quite easy to work. The design is based on the simple one-patch idea, and consists of a series of small squares positioned to form a diamond-shape pattern. I have used just three colours that can be altered, if you wish, to suit the colour scheme of your dolls' house.

Materials
- 27tpi evenweave linen or similar
- Tapestry needle, size 26 or 28
- Stranded cotton, as listed in key
- Narrow ribbon for edging
- Backing fabric
- Small amount of stuffing or tiny beads

Stranded cotton

▢	.........DMC 369
▢	.........DMC 958
▢	.........DMC 316

Design size ....1in (25mm) square

Stitch ....tent

Stitch count..30 x 30

Stitch size ....worked over every thread

Number of strands 2

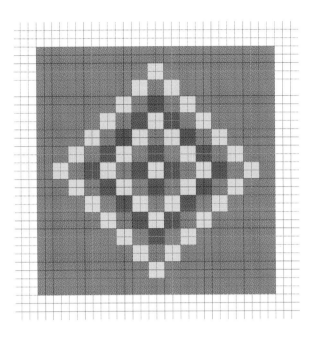

Working method

Mount your fabric in a frame (see pages 17–19), then begin by embroidering the four stitches for the central square. Work outwards, completing the four green squares, then the eight pink squares, and so on, until you have completed all of the squares. Finally, work the background, ensuring all your stitches lie in the same direction. Finish and make up your cushion as described on pages 40–41.

Variations

This cushion can easily be enlarged, either by working extra rows of squares or by working on a fabric with fewer threads to the inch (tpi). For example, on 20tpi fabric your cushion will be approximately 1½in (38mm) square, but in this case you will need three strands of thread in your needle to cover the fabric. Try also continuing the rows of squares out to each corner until all the corners are filled and there is no longer any background. Alternatively, work each 'diamond' of squares in a different colour for a psychedelic look!

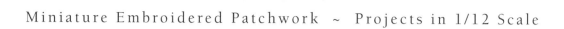

DIFFICULTY
RATING

Blue and Cream Nine-Patch

This elegant nine-patch cushion uses just three subtle colours. In addition to suiting a modern chair, as shown here, it would look well on a Georgian-style chair or sofa in the drawing room of your dolls' house. The cushion is fun to work, with very little counting required, but be sure to leave one thread of fabric between each completed square for the darker dividing lines.

Materials

- ◆ 27tpi evenweave fabric
- ◆ Tapestry needle, size 26 or 28
- ◆ Stranded cotton, as listed in key
- ◆ Short length of wool for the edging
- ◆ Backing fabric
- ◆ Small amount of stuffing or tiny beads

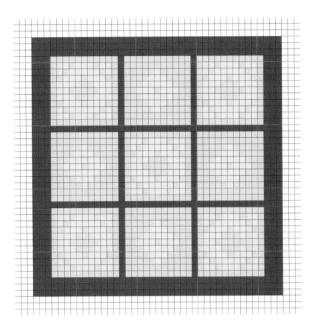

Stranded cotton

▮	DMC 931
▯	DMC 677
▯	DMC 3752

Design size ....1½in (38mm) square

Stitch ....tent

Stitch count.....................................41 x 41

Stitch size ....worked over every thread

Number of strands 2

Working method

For best results your fabric should be mounted in a frame (see pages 17–19). The design can then be worked in any direction, but you may find it easier to start at the top left or right corner. Completing one patchwork square at a time, work along and down. Leave one thread of your fabric between each completed square for the darker lines of tent stitch. When all the squares and dividing lines have been worked, create a border by embroidering three rows of tent stitch around the design. Finish and make up as described on pages 40–41.

Variations

Just three colours have been used for this cushion, but a completely different effect can be achieved by using more colours, perhaps from opposite sides of the colour wheel. Try your own colour combination for a unique result. (For advice on colour, see Colour Guidelines, pages 22–23.)

The design can also be repeated to make a beautiful single or double bedcover. (See Adapting Projects, pages 130–131.)

DIFFICULTY RATING

Octagonal Pattern

I have taken the basic octagonal shape, so often used in pieced patchwork, to create the design for this cushion. Although it is worked in fairly muted colours, the bright edging brings it to life. You will find it quick and easy to stitch, and, as there are only three colours, not much needle threading is required.

Materials
- 25tpi evenweave fabric
- Tapestry needle, size 26 or 28
- Stranded cotton, as listed in key
- Short length of wool for the edging
- Backing fabric
- Small amount of stuffing or tiny beads

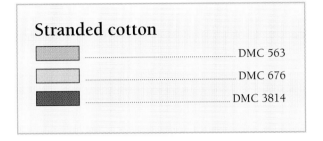

Stranded cotton

▭	.... DMC 563
▭	.... DMC 676
▭	.... DMC 3814

Design size.............................1¼ x 1⅜in (32 x 35mm)

Stitch ....tent

Stitch count..32 x 34

Stitch size ....worked over every thread

Number of strands 2

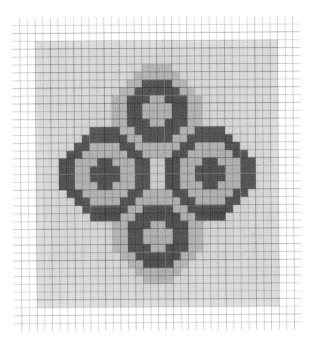

Working method

Mount your fabric in a frame (see pages 17–19), and then begin by embroidering the 12 inner stitches of one octagon. Next, work the stitches that adjoin it with the contrasting colour, then work the outer stitches. When you have completed one octagon, move on to the next, until all four have been worked. By working one octagon at a time you will find there is very little counting to do and therefore less chance of misplacing a stitch. Lastly, work the background, ensuring all your stitches lie in the same direction. Finish and make up as described on pages 40–41.

Variations

An alternative effect can be achieved by working each of the octagons in a different colour. Bright colours, for instance, would make this a lovely cushion for a nursery.

You could also use the design to cover a stool top, perhaps in shades of blue and cream for a bathroom, or pastel shades for a bedroom. Alternatively, repeat the basic octagonal design to create a much larger item for your dolls' house, such as a carpet or bedcover. (For advice, see Adapting Projects, pages 130–131.)

DIFFICULTY
RATING

Flower Basket

This pretty little cushion is very straightforward to work and requires just three colours. It would be suitable for many rooms in the dolls' house, including a sitting room, drawing room or bedroom. The pattern is made up of a series of triangles in varying sizes – simplicity itself, but very effective, and you will probably find you can complete the embroidery in an evening.

Materials
◆ 25tpi evenweave fabric
◆ Tapestry needle, size 26 or 28
◆ Stranded cotton, as listed in key
◆ Short length of wool for the edging
◆ Backing fabric
◆ Small amount of stuffing or tiny beads

Stranded cotton

![swatch]	.... DMC 352
![swatch]	.... DMC 472
![swatch]	.... DMC 3740

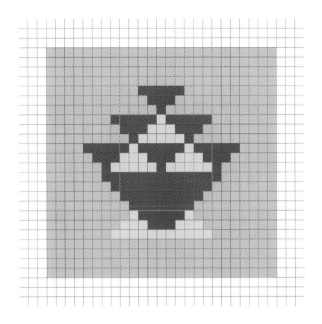

Design size ....1in (25mm) square

Stitch ....tent

Stitch count.....................................25 x 24

Stitch size ....worked over every thread

Number of strands 2

Working method

Mount your fabric in a frame (see pages 17–19), then begin by embroidering the small brown triangle at the top of the design. Work downwards, completing each brown triangle. Next, work the lime green triangles, and lastly the background. Ensure all your stitches lie in the same direction. Finish and make up as described on pages 40–41.

Variations

You can embroider this pattern several times to make a set of cushions, maybe varying the colours for the flower baskets. Alternatively, you may like to enlarge the cushion, by either extending the background colour by a few rows in each direction or by using a fabric with fewer threads to the inch (tpi). For example, the same design worked on 20tpi will give a finished size of approximately 1¼in (32mm) and on 18tpi approximately 1½in (38mm). Remember to use sufficient threads in your needle to cover the fabric. (See Adapting Projects, pages 130–131.)

You could also consider using this design for a small, square stool top, perhaps to go under a lady's dressing table. In this case, you could either make a stool to fit the embroidery size (see Finishing & Making Up, Stools, page 54) or buy a ready-made stool which you can then cover with your embroidery.

**DIFFICULTY
RATING**

Friendship Star

This little cushion would look perfect in the drawing room of your dolls' house or in a wood-panelled library. The design is simply made by repeating the patchwork pattern, known as Friendship Star, four times.

The cushion is worked on 35tpi fabric, so it requires a little more patience than the other cushions, but I think you will find it worth the effort. And, as there are only two colours, not much needle threading is required.

Materials
- 35tpi evenweave linen
- Embroidery needle, size 10
- Stranded cotton, as listed in key
- Backing fabric
- Small amount of stuffing or tiny beads

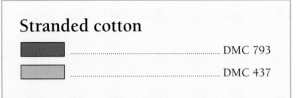

Stranded cotton

.... DMC 793

.... DMC 437

Design size ....1in (25mm) square

Stitch ....tent

Stitch count...34 x 34

Stitch size ....worked over every thread

Number of strands 1

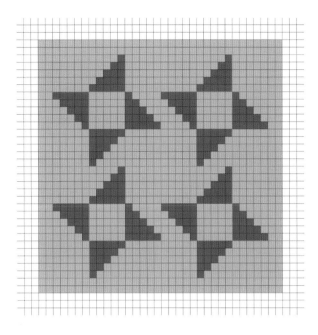

Working method

Mount your fabric in a frame (see pages 17–19), then begin by embroidering the blue triangles, completing one star at a time. When you have completed all the stars, work the background, ensuring all your stitches lie in the same direction. Make up and finish as described on pages 40–41.

Variations

You may prefer to work this design on a fabric where the holes are a little easier to see! If so, try working on 25tpi for a cushion approximately 1½in (38mm) square, or 18tpi for a large floor cushion approximately 2in (51mm) square. Remember to use sufficient strands of thread in your needle to cover the fabric.

**DIFFICULTY
RATING**

Eight-Triangle

This is a straightforward pattern to work, and you will probably find you can embroider it in an evening. Like the Flower Basket and Friendship Star cushions, the design of this delicate cushion consists entirely of triangles. I have used a pale, pastel colour for the background, but I think the design would work equally well with a dark background and perhaps slightly lighter shades for the triangles; it would then be especially suitable for a library or study in the dolls' house.

Materials
- ◆ 27tpi evenweave fabric
- ◆ Tapestry needle, size 26 or 28
- ◆ Stranded cotton, as listed in key
- ◆ Narrow ribbon for the edging
- ◆ Backing fabric
- ◆ Small amount of stuffing or tiny beads

Stranded cotton

▉	DMC 718
▉	DMC 553
▉	DMC 554
▉	DMC 605
▉	DMC 3752
▉	DMC 958
▉	DMC 603
▉	DMC 3328

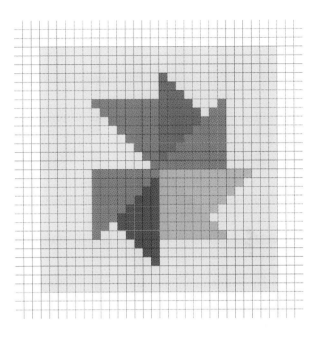

Design size ....1in (25mm) square

Stitch ....tent

Stitch count...28 x 28

Stitch size ....worked over every thread

Number of strands 2

Working method

Mount your fabric in a frame (see pages 17–19), then begin by embroidering one of the triangles at the top, working clockwise or anti-clockwise until they are all complete. Although the back of your work will not be seen, it is good practice to finish off each thread under the back of the stitches that are in the same colour. Lastly, work the background, ensuring your stitches lie in the same direction. Finish and make up as described on pages 40–41.

Variations

This cushion can easily be enlarged either by extending the background colour by a few rows in each direction, by re-designing the cushion with larger triangles, or by using fabric with fewer threads to the inch (tpi). For example, the same design worked on 18tpi would give a finished size of approximately 1½in (38mm); but, remember, you would then need at least three strands of thread in your needle. Alternatively, this design would look pretty if repeated three times along the top of a footstool, working on a fine 35tpi fabric. (See Adapting Projects, pages 130–131.)

DIFFICULTY
RATING

Roman Stripes

I have embroidered this cushion to match the Roman Stripes rug on pages 58–60, although I have given it a slightly different appearance by using a green edging. In pieced patchwork, the stripes are formed using varying lengths of narrow strips of material, sewn together to form a triangle, which, in turn, are then sewn to another triangle of material to form a square block. This design is easily represented in tent stitch, as long as the stripes are formed from bottom left to top right. In case you wish to design some for yourself, don't be tempted to have the stripes going in the other direction – if using tent stitch you will end up with a series of dashes and no distinct stripes!

Materials

- 25tpi evenweave fabric
- Tapestry needle, size 26 or 28
- Stranded cotton, as listed in key
- Three short lengths of wool for the edging
- Backing fabric
- Small amount of stuffing or tiny beads

Stranded cotton

	DMC 223
	DMC 437
	DMC 501
	DMC 522
	DMC 613
	DMC 370
	DMC 778

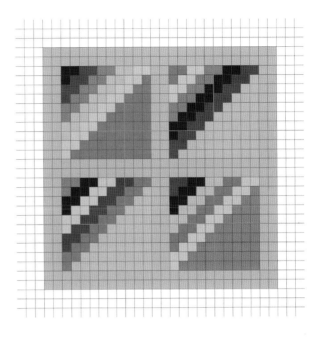

Design size ....1in (25mm) square

Stitch ....tent

Stitch count..26 x 26

Stitch size ....worked over every thread

Number of strands 2

Working method

First mount your fabric in a frame (see pages 17–19), then begin by embroidering one of the large triangles. Work each of the stripes underneath the triangle until you have completed that block. Work the other three blocks, remembering to leave two rows free between each block. You can then work the borders and dividing lines, ensuring all your stitches lie in the same direction. Finish and make up as described on pages 40–41.

Variations

You could try working the design twice on a stool top, giving an overall size of approximately 2 x 1in (51 x 25mm). In this case, you would not need to work four rows of the background colour where the blocks meet, only two.

Finishing and Making Up

I have yet to meet anyone who actually enjoys the making-up part of miniature embroidery, and no one can deny that making up cushions in 1/12 scale is a fiddly business! However, you will have spent considerable time and effort getting this far, so it really is worth taking the trouble to make up the work as carefully as possible.

Firstly, remove your embroidery from the frame and, if necessary, pull it gently into shape. If your embroidery is badly distorted you may need to block it (see Getting Started, Blocking, page 21). If you wish, the embroidery can be lightly pressed by placing it face down on a clean towel, then pressing gently with a warm iron.

Next, trim the fabric, leaving a margin of approximately five holes from the embroidery, then cut a piece of matching or contrasting backing material to the same overall size. Use thin material for the backing, preferably one that does not fray too easily and is not overly slippery; for example, I find that dress-lining material has a mind of its own! Lightweight cotton is easiest to handle and therefore ideal. For a special look use pure silk.

Now turn the edges of the embroidered fabric under so that the outside stitches lie along the edges, and then crease the fabric slightly between your fingers and thumb. Make similar turnings on your backing fabric. If you wish, cut away a little of the excess fabric at the corners of both pieces. They should now be the same size with neat square corners.

Place the WRONG sides together and carefully join them by using an oversewing stitch in a matching sewing thread, keeping the stitches as small as possible and leaving a small opening along one edge. Be careful to keep it 'square'. I sometimes find it useful to hold the two pieces together with a fine lace pin, which will not mark the embroidery.

NB: I do not recommend sewing the embroidery and backing fabric right sides together, as tiny cushions are very difficult to turn out to the right side and, in doing so, you risk fraying both fabrics.

When your two pieces of fabric are joined, tease a small amount of soft stuffing into minute wisps (tiny beads also make a good filling) and carefully fill the cushion, making sure it goes right into the corners (a small blunt-ended tool is useful for this). Cushions look more natural in dolls' houses if they are not overfilled. When you are pleased with the effect, sew the remaining edges together.

As long as your joining stitches don't show, the edges of your cushion can be left plain, as in the Friendship Star cushion (pages 34–35). Alternatively, they can be decorated with very narrow braid, ribbon, cord, wool, plaited wool or plaited stranded cotton.

To make a plait you will need either three lengths of 6ply stranded cotton or three lengths of wool, which should be at least 4in (100mm) longer than the total length of your four edges. Knot the three lengths together at one end and attach it to something heavy, or ask someone to hold the knotted end for you. Now simply plait the three lengths together, trying to keep the plait as even as possible. When you get near the end, make another knot close to the plaiting.

To attach your trimming, apply a very small amount of fabric glue along one edge of your cushion with a cocktail stick as an applicator, then lay the

trimming onto it. Let each edge dry before gluing the next. Finish by cutting the trimming to allow a tiny overlap and securing it with glue.

When using a single strand of wool, as with the Flower Basket cushion on pages 32–33, you can make 'tassels' by cutting four pieces of wool, each a little longer than the edges of the cushion, attaching them one at a time, then fraying the edges. Trim the 'tassels' to a length you like. Make sure you glue right to the corners of the cushion.

You may prefer to couch your trimmings onto the cushion edges. If so, lay your trimming along one edge of the cushion and, with matching or contrasting sewing thread, oversew along its length, going right to the corner. Continue working around all sides of the cushion, keeping your stitches fairly close while being careful not to pull them too tightly, as this will result in the edges looking wrinkled. Finally, overlap slightly at the end and secure well with your thread.

Chapter 3
Stools

A stool can provide a useful and decorative addition to many rooms in the dolls' house. You will find that the the stool tops in this chapter are varied, while still retaining the patchwork theme. Each can be used for a dressing-table stool, footstool or, in the case of the plainer 'one-patch' stool, for the kitchen or scullery.

DIFFICULTY RATING

Tumbling Blocks

Many of you will recognize the Tumbling Blocks pattern, so often used in pieced patchwork, where the effect is achieved by a clever mix of materials, carefully placed to create the effect of three-dimensional blocks. This illusionary design is difficult to create in miniature embroidery but, after much experimentation with different colour values, the result is this little stool.

The actual working of the pattern is not too demanding, but I have given it a difficulty rating of two because there are twenty-one colours and therefore a lot of needle threading! However, the effect is worth the effort, and when I take this stool to miniature embroidery fairs, it is frequently the first item to be picked up and looked at.

Materials
◆ 27tpi evenweave fabric
◆ Tapestry needle, size 26 or 28
◆ Stranded cotton, as listed in key

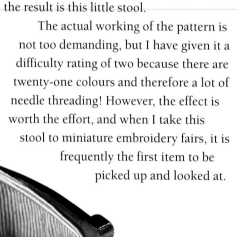

Stranded cotton

▨	DMC 718
▨	DMC 677
▨	DMC 742
▨	DMC 307
▨	DMC 550
▨	DMC 3608
▨	DMC 3809
▨	DMC 3811
▨	DMC 501
▨	DMC 793
▨	DMC 336
▨	DMC 3752
▨	DMC 3814
▨	DMC 472
▨	DMC 563
▨	DMC 352
▨	DMC 900
▨	DMC 3779
▨	DMC 605
▨	DMC 818
▨	DMC 961

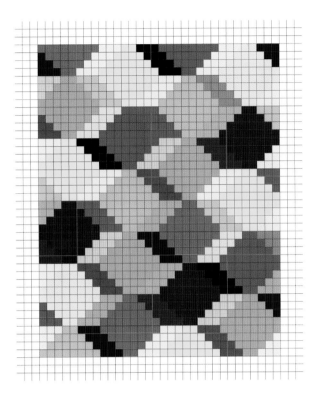

Design size.............................1½ x 1¼in (38 x 32mm)

Stitch ....tent

Stitch count.....................................40 x 32

Stitch size ....worked over every thread

Number of strands 2

Working method

Mount the fabric in a frame (see pages 17–19), then begin by embroidering one of the colours at the top left or right corner. Gradually progress across and down, working each colour as you get to it – that way, there is very little counting to do and you don't risk misplacing a block of colour. It helps to have several needles already threaded in different colours. Finish and make up as described on page 54.

Variations

This is one of the more difficult patterns to enlarge. However, you could work a border in one of the colours already used, or perhaps a contrasting colour, to help it fit a stool you wish to cover. Alternatively, you could reduce its size by removing a small section of the pattern from either end and using the embroidery for a cushion.

DIFFICULTY
RATING

Diamond Pattern

This delicate little stool top is worked on a 40tpi silk gauze, which has allowed for several repeats of the design in a relatively small area. I have used a fine random-dyed silk thread to work the pattern, which gives it a shaded appearance along its length, and a fine silk in a solid colour for the background.

Silk gauze is lovely to work on but it is abrasive, so I would advise using short lengths of thread in your needle – no more than 7in (178mm) – otherwise the thread will gradually fray as you push it backwards and forwards through the gauze. Silk gauze has one great advantage over cotton or linen evenweave fabrics: the threads of the gauze are very fine, therefore the holes are larger – and, of course, it is the holes you need to see!

Materials

- ◆ 40tpi silk gauze
- ◆ Quilting needle, size 10
- ◆ Fine random-dyed silk thread for pattern
- ◆ Fine silk thread, in solid colour for background

Stranded cotton

Not applicable for this pattern.

Design size	1¾ x 1⅛in (44 x 28mm)
Stitch	tent
Stitch count	60 x 42
Stitch size	worked over every thread
Number of strands	1

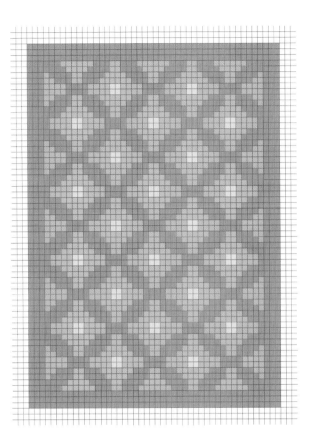

Working method

The colours in the chart are an indication of the overall colours of silks I chose. When using random-dyed threads, you will probably find that each of the colour variations along the length of the skein are several inches long, as they will not have been dyed for miniature embroidery. This means that you could work quite a large area in miniature and not notice any colour variation. To avoid this happening, be selective in the length of thread you use, and each time you re-thread your needle, cut a short length where there is some variation that pleases you. You will find it easier not to wind your random-dyed threads onto a cardboard spool, but to use them straight from the skein so you can see how the colours vary.

First mount your fabric in a frame. I found a card frame was ideal for this project (see pages 18–19). Now work the pattern, starting at the top left or right corner. You will need to count the gauze threads carefully between each pattern shape to ensure correct placement. When the pattern has been worked, fill in the background with a solid colour that will give greater definition to the pattern. Finish and make up as described on page 54.

Variations

This pattern could be reduced by six stitches at either end to make a very pretty set of cushions. By using random-dyed silks, each one would be slightly different.

DIFFICULTY
RATING

Single-Patch

Simple patterns can often be very pleasing, and with this stool top each square is just five stitches across and down. The whole top can be embroidered in an evening.

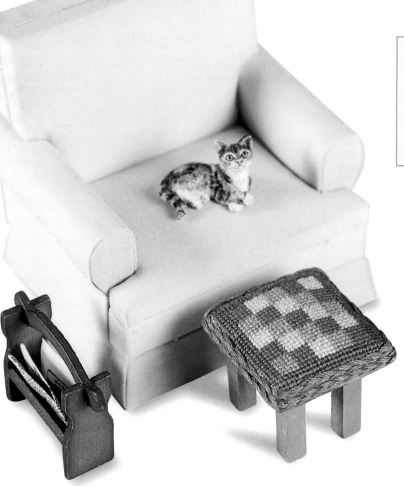

Materials
♦ 27tpi evenweave fabric
♦ Tapestry needle, size 26 or 28
♦ Stranded cotton, as listed in key

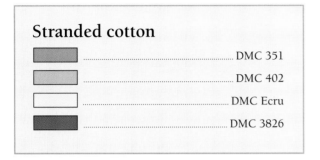

Stranded cotton

▬	DMC 351
▬	DMC 402
▭	DMC Ecru
▬	DMC 3826

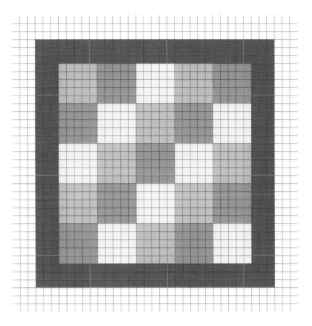

Design size .... 1¼in (32mm) square

Stitch .... tent

Stitch count .... 31 x 31

Stitch size .... worked over every thread

Number of strands 2

Working method

Mount your fabric in a frame (see pages 17–19), then begin at the top left or right corner, working one square at a time. Progress across and down until all the squares are complete. Finally, work three rows all around in the border colour. Finish and make up as described on page 54.

Variations

You can make the pattern fit the top of an existing stool by reducing or increasing the number of rows in the border. Choose your own colours for a completely different look, and use the pattern to produce a matching cushion.

**DIFFICULTY
RATING**

Random-Patch

Random patchwork is the name given to a method of creating a length of material by sewing together a selection of random shapes and colours of material in no particular order. This usually results in a highly patterned, unique piece of fabric, which can be used for clothing, bedcovers and cushions, etc.

I decided to include a stool top using the concept of Random patchwork, and I must say I thoroughly enjoyed designing and working it. I have incorporated four lines of a single colour throughout the pattern to give it an element of order!

Materials
- ◆ 27tpi evenweave fabric
- ◆ Tapestry needle, size 26 or 28
- ◆ Stranded cotton, as listed in key

Stranded cotton

![swatch]	DMC 334
![swatch]	DMC 350
![swatch]	DMC 554
![swatch]	DMC 815
![swatch]	DMC 3773

Design size.................................1½ x ⅛in (38 x 28mm)

Stitch ....tent

Stitch count...40 x 30

Stitch size ....worked over every thread

Number of strands 2

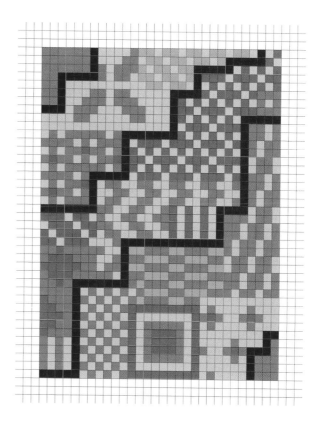

Working method

First mount your fabric in a frame (see pages 17–19).
The design can then be worked in any direction, but
you may find it easier to start at the top left or right
corner. Work along and down, completing one
random patch at a time. Remember to leave a space
for the four zigzag lines, or work them in as you go.
Ensure all your stitches lie in the same direction.
Finish and make up as described on page 54.

Variations

If necessary, this design can be enlarged to fit a ready-
made stool by using one of the colours to embroider a
few rows of border. You can also extend the pattern to
make, for instance, a window seat cover, either by
repeating it again or by adding your own random
patches. The designs for random patchwork are
limited only by your imagination, so do experiment
for yourself, perhaps using single-colour patches
instead of patterned.

DIFFICULTY
RATING

Octagonal Pattern

The octagon is a shape often used in pieced patchwork, so I have decided to use it in the design of this brightly coloured stool top. It is not too difficult to work, as each octagon is in a solid colour and the spacing of them is fairly clear, so very little counting is necessary. The stool would look pretty in the bedroom of a dolls' house, perhaps on a pink carpet.

Materials

◆ 27tpi evenweave fabric
◆ Tapestry needle, size 26 or 28
◆ Stranded cotton, as listed in key

Stranded cotton

![]	DMC 502
![]	DMC 3819
![]	DMC 553
![]	DMC 961
![]	DMC 3803
![]	DMC Ecru

Design size .... 1¾ x 1in (44 x 25mm)

Stitch .... tent

Stitch count .... 45 x 29

Stitch size .... worked over every thread

Number of strands 2

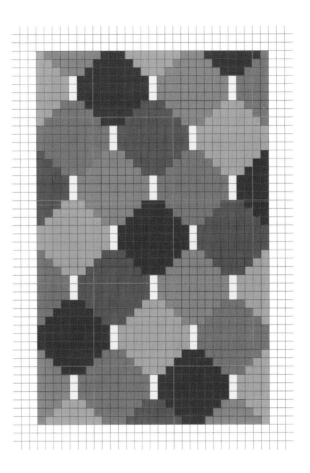

Working method

First mount your fabric in a frame (see pages 17–19). As with many of the projects in this book, you can then start the embroidery anywhere and the result will be the same, but I usually find it easier to start at the top left or right corner. Work one octagon at a time, gradually progressing along and down. When all the octagons are complete, use Ecru thread to fill in the three stitches between each one. Finish and make up as described on page 54.

Variations

By using six alternative colours the effect of the stool will be entirely different – just make sure the colours you choose are far enough apart in the colour spectrum for the pattern to show. (See Colour Guidelines, pages 22–23.) This design can also be easily extended to create a single or double bedcover (see Adapting Projects, page 130–131).

Finishing and Making Up

Remove your embroidery from the frame and, if necessary, pull it gently into shape. If your embroidery has been badly distorted you may need to block it (see Blocking, page 21). If you wish, the embroidery can be lightly pressed by placing it face down on a clean towel and pressing it gently with a warm iron.

When you are satisfied with the shape, trim the embroidery, leaving enough of a margin for turnings. Next, cut a piece of card and stripwood the same size as the finished embroidery. Using a little fabric glue, stick a small amount of wadding or four layers of a soft fabric onto the card. Lay your embroidery face up on the wadding and turn under the spare fabric on one long side, attaching it to the back of the card with fabric glue. Repeat the process for the other long side and then also for both ends, sticking the corners down as flatly and neatly as possible.

Apply a little stain, paint or polish to the underside of your stripwood, and allow it to dry. Place your embroidery-covered card onto the unfinished side of your stripwood and glue, holding the edges until they are stuck. You can now attach either four matching wooden beads (ideal for a footstool) or four ready-

Materials for making a stool
- A piece of card (postcard thickness)
- A piece of stripwood
- Four wooden beads or four 1/12 scale wooden legs
- Narrow trimming, such as braid or ribbon
- Fabric glue

made cabriole-style legs (which are available commercially) to your stool.

Finish your stool by applying a tiny amount of fabric glue to one edge at a time, then attaching your chosen trimming. Allow each edge to dry thoroughly before doing the next. Where the trimming meets, allow a tiny overlap.

If you have a ready-made stool and it has a covered top, carefully remove the top and make a card template to fit. Proceed as above by attaching your embroidery to the card and then the card to the stool top.

NB: If your embroidery is the wrong size for the stool, see Adapting Projects, pages 130–131.

Chapter 4

Rugs

S oft furnishings add colour and comfort to a room, and none more so than rugs. Although pieced patchwork does not lend itself to full-size floor coverings, I have adapted some of the well-known patchwork patterns to create four very different embroidered rugs for your dolls' house.

In this chapter you will find an elegant rug embroidered in the Roman Stripes pattern, the 'Baubles' rug, which has a pattern made up of repeating octagonal shapes, a single-patch rug that would be suitable for a nursery, and a Random-Patch rug. I have also included two bathroom mats that are quick and easy to work. I hope some (or all!) of these rugs will enhance your dolls' house.

DIFFICULTY RATING

Roman Stripes

The original idea for this rug came from a large carpet I once saw in a store, and I am pleased with the way the traditional Roman Stripes patchwork pattern has converted so well to a miniature rug. The double border gives it an Italianate feel, and it looks lovely in the drawing room of my dolls' house, set off by a few elegant pieces of furniture around it.

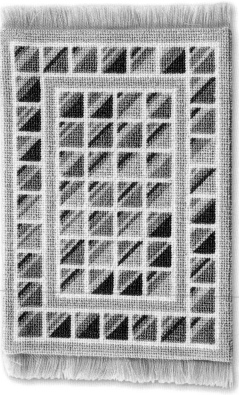

Materials
- 25tpi evenweave fabric
- Tapestry needle, size 26 or 28
- Stranded cotton, as listed in key
- Fine material for fringing

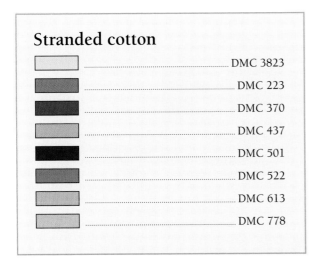

Stranded cotton

	DMC 3823
	DMC 223
	DMC 370
	DMC 437
	DMC 501
	DMC 522
	DMC 613
	DMC 778

Design size	5¼ x 3¾in (133 x 95mm)
Stitch	tent
Stitch count	132 x 96
Stitch size	worked over every thread
Number of strands	2

Working method

First mount your fabric in a frame (see pages 17–19), then begin by embroidering the top left or right corner square of the inner section. Work the large triangle first, then the five colour bands. I recommend working the yellow divisional lines as you go, so that you don't forget to leave space for them – it will also help with the counting. When the twenty-eight inner squares are complete, work the inner yellow and gold borders, then the outer squares. Finally, work the outer yellow and gold borders, ensuring all your stitches lie in the same direction. Finish and make up as described on page 73.

Variations

Instead of the relatively understated colours I have used, try working this design in bright contrasting colours for a really contemporary look. The large triangles can be worked in the same colour or in different colours, mixed randomly as I have done.

For a less ambitious project, just work the centre section, perhaps on a lower count of fabric. In this case, remember to use more strands of thread in your needle to cover the fabric. When this pattern is worked on 18tpi fabric it produces an overall rug size of approximately 7½ x 5½in (189 x 140mm), and if only the centre part with a border is worked on this scale the size will be approximately 5 x 3in (127 x 76mm).

Matching cushions can be worked by taking just four of the squares from the rug, as I have done for the Roman Stripes cushion on pages 38–39. (See Adapting Projects, pages 130–131.)

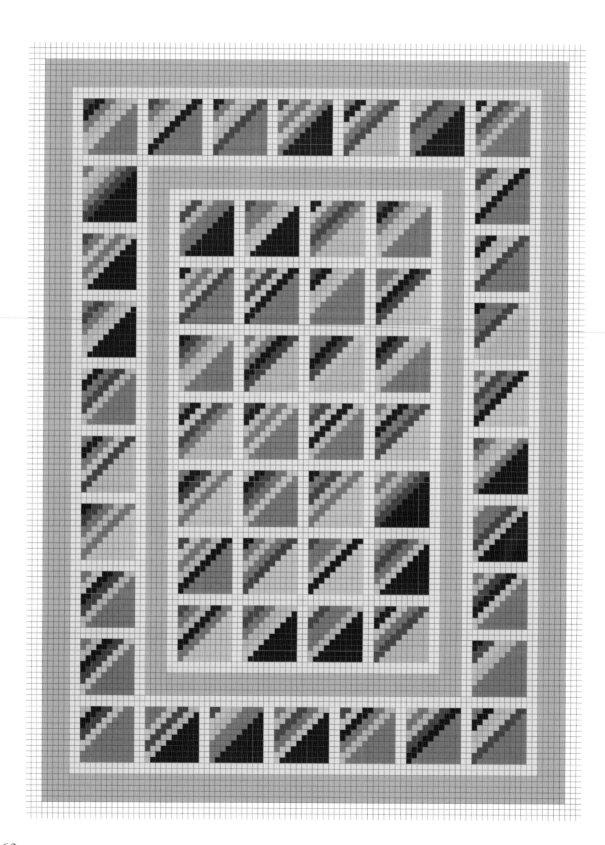

DIFFICULTY
RATING

Random-Patch

When designing this rug I had in mind the memory of a rag-rug my grandmother had on her kitchen floor when I was a child. It was dark with plenty of black in it, but I thought that would be a little 'heavy' for most dolls' houses. Instead, I chose to use brighter colours, and in each case had one thread of the colour shown on the chart in my needle and one of DMC 3740 as a mixer. Having more than one colour in your needle at a time is always fascinating, as the mixer colour can have different effects on the other colours, so you never quite know what the finished result will be.

Materials

- ◆ 25tpi evenweave fabric
- ◆ Tapestry needle, size 26 or 28
- ◆ Stranded cotton as listed in key, and mixer colour DMC 3740

Stranded cotton

▬	DMC 722
▬	DMC 676
▬	DMC 223
▬	DMC 355
▬	DMC 501
▬	DMC 523

Design size............................4⅜ x 3⅜in (112 x 86mm)

Stitch ....tent

Stitch count...108 x 83

Stitch size ....worked over every thread

Number of strands........2 (one from chart, one mixer)

Working method

Mount your fabric in a frame (see pages 17–19), then begin embriodering at the top left or right corner. Work along and down, completing one random patch before going on to the next. When all the patches are complete, work the four border rows. Finish and make up as described on page 73.

Variations

Try your own colour combinations, but remember to use fairly bright main colours so that the mixer colour shows.

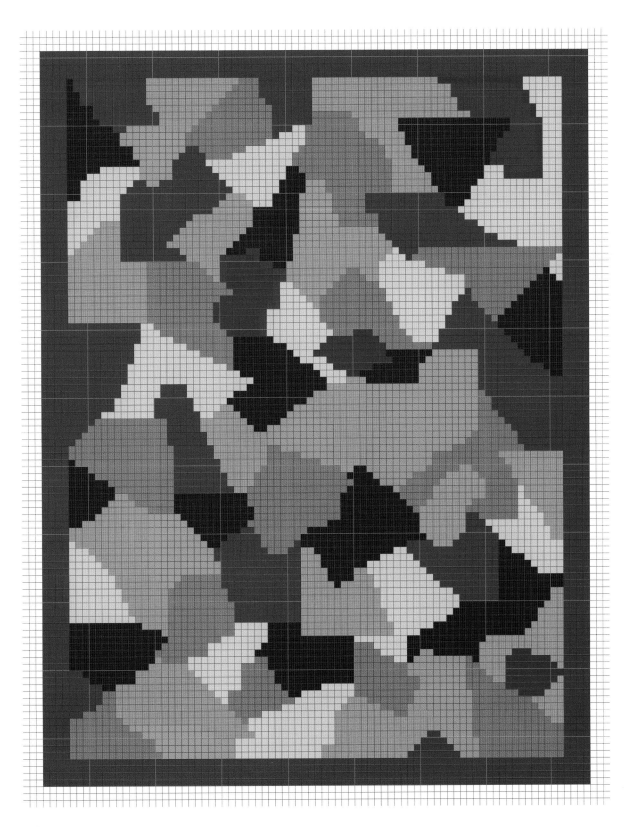

**DIFFICULTY
RATING**

Baubles

When I designed this bright little rug, using the popular octagonal patchwork shape, I didn't realize the finished result would remind me of coloured baubles! I guess this effect is due to having used random-dyed silk threads, which give an iridescent look to the shapes. Of course, if you prefer, you can use solid colours when working the rug.

Materials
◆ 24tpi coin net
◆ Tapestry needle, size 24 or 26
◆ Selection of random-dyed fine silks
◆ Fine material for fringing

Stranded cotton

Not applicable for this pattern.

Design size ....4 x 3in (102 x 76mm)

Stitch ....tent

Stitch count..96 x 72

Stitch size ....worked over every thread

Number of strands 2

Working method

The colours shown on the chart are to give you an indication only of the overall colour of the silks I chose. When using this type of thread, you will probably find that each of the colour variations along the length of the skein is several inches long, as it will not have been dyed for miniature embroidery. This means that you could work quite a large area in miniature and not notice any colour variation. To avoid this happening, be selective in the length of thread you use, and each time you re-thread your needle, cut a short length where there is some variation that pleases you. You will find it easier not to wind your random-dyed skeins onto a cardboard spool, but to use the thread straight from the skein so that you can see how the colours vary.

For best results, mount your fabric in a frame (see pages 17–19). The pattern can then be worked in any direction, completing one set of four octagons at a time to avoid too much thread changing. Careful counting is required to avoid misplacing the shapes. When all are worked, fill in the background and, lastly, work the border. Finish and make up as described on page 73.

Variations

By omitting the fringing, this pattern can be used as a colourful, contemporary wall hanging or extended and used as a bedcover. (See Adapting Projects, pages 130–131.)

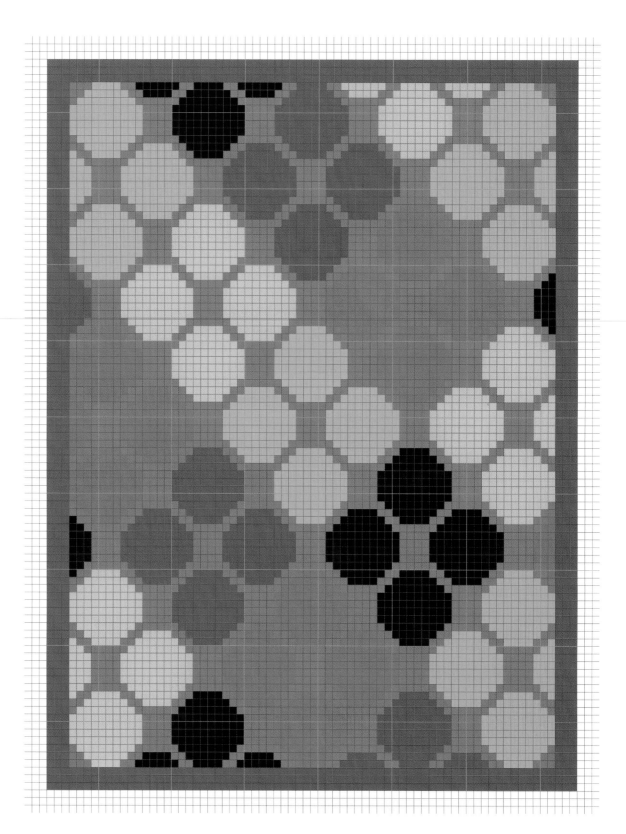

DIFFICULTY
RATING

Single-Patch

This small 'single-patch' rug is vibrant and fun, so it is probably most suited to a child's bedroom. I have used the three primary colours of red, blue and yellow, with the addition of brown and green. The rug was quick and easy to work and is the sort of project one can take on a long train or coach journey, as there is no need to keep referring to the pattern and very little counting is required.

Materials
♦ 24tpi coin net
♦ Tapestry needle, size 24 or 26
♦ Stranded cotton, as listed in key

Stranded cotton

▬	.... DMC 309
▬	.... DMC 334
▬	.... DMC 501
▬	.... DMC 632
▬	.... DMC 676

Design size.............................3¼ x 2⅜in (82 x 61mm)

Stitch ....tent

Stitch count..78 x 58

Stitch size ....worked over every thread

Number of strands 2

Working method

For best results, mount your fabric in a frame (see pages 17–19). To avoid too much needle threading, I recommend working the squares in their diagonal rows, rather than horizontally. You can either start in a corner and work outwards, or start with one of the longest rows and work outwards to either side of it. When all the squares are complete, work the four border rows. Finish and make up as described on page 73.

Variations

Try working the pattern in gentle pastel colours for a completely different effect. The rug can also be easily made larger by working more rows of squares along and down or by having a wider border.

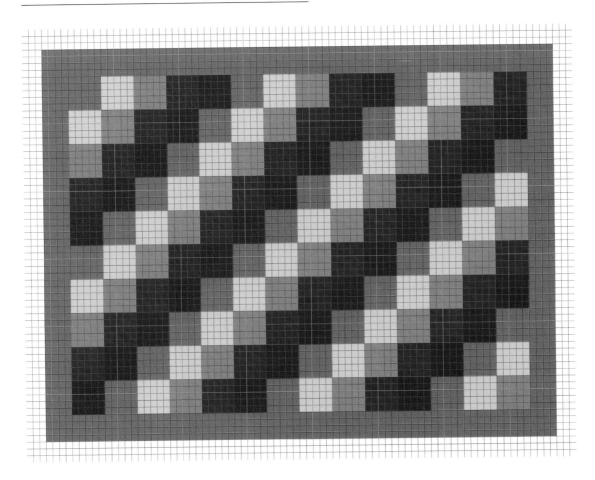

DIFFICULTY
RATING

Blue and Cream Bath Mat

I think this little bathroom mat illustrates how easy it is to create a pleasing pattern from very simple shapes. The pattern is made up entirely of triangles, with just one square at each corner, and it is quick and easy to work. If you wish, you can alter the colours to coordinate with the colour scheme in the bathroom of your dolls' house.

Materials
- ◆ 24tpi coin net
- ◆ Tapestry needle, size 24 or 26
- ◆ Stranded cotton, as listed in key

Stranded cotton

▬	.... DMC 334
▬	.... DMC 336
▭	.... DMC Ecru

Design size ....2¾ x 2in (70 x 51mm)

Stitch ....tent

Stitch count.....................................68 x 48

Stitch size ....worked over every thread

Number of strands 2

Working method

Mount your fabric in a frame (see pages 17–19). Begin by working each dark blue triangle, then the light blue triangles. Alternatively, you may prefer to thread two needles and work both colours as you go. When the pattern is complete, work the background, ensuring the stitches lie in the same direction. Finish and make up as described on page 73.

Variations

This pattern can be easily extended to make a larger rug for any room in your dolls' house. Or it could, for instance, be worked on a fine 40tpi silk gauze for a stool top. (See Adapting Projects, pages 130–131.)

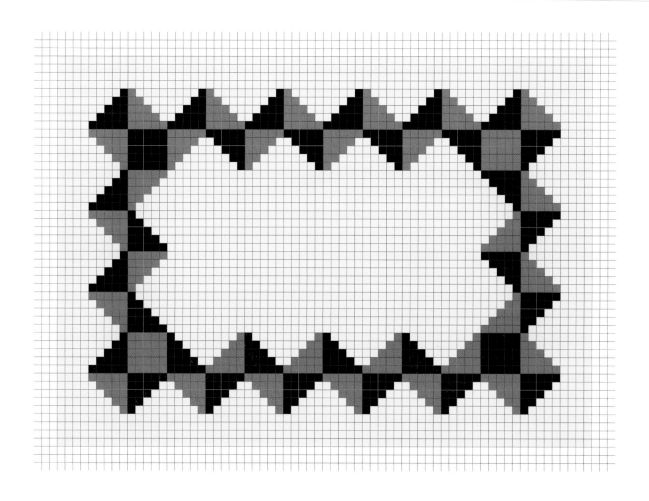

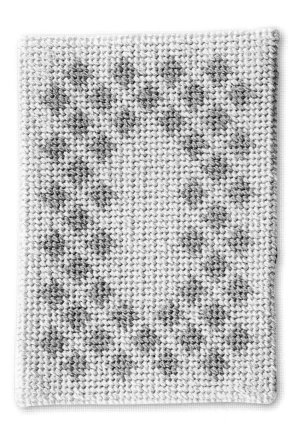

DIFFICULTY RATING

Yellow Bath Mat

This simple diamond-shape pattern makes an attractive mat for a bathroom or kitchen and is very easily worked. I have chosen fairly soft colours, but it would also look good in stronger colours, such as navy with an off-white background or maroon with a pale pink background. You may wish to alter the colours to suit the colour scheme in your dolls' house.

Materials
- ◆ 24tpi coin net
- ◆ Tapestry needle, size 24 or 26
- ◆ Stranded cotton, as listed in key

Stranded cotton

▬	DMC 783
▬	DMC 677

Design size.............................2½ x 1⅞in (64 x 47mm)

Stitch ....tent

Stitch count..61 x 45

Stitch size ....worked over every thread

Number of strands 2

Working method

Mount the fabric in a frame (see pages 17–19), then begin by embroidering the pattern shapes, making sure you place them correctly. Once they are complete, work the background, ensuring all your stitches lie in the same direction. Finish and make up as described on page 73.

Variations

Try extending the pattern from the centre to make a hall runner, or work the pattern on 18tpi canvas, which will result in a rug that measures approximately 3½ x 2½in (89 x 64mm). (See Adapting Projects, pages 130–131.)

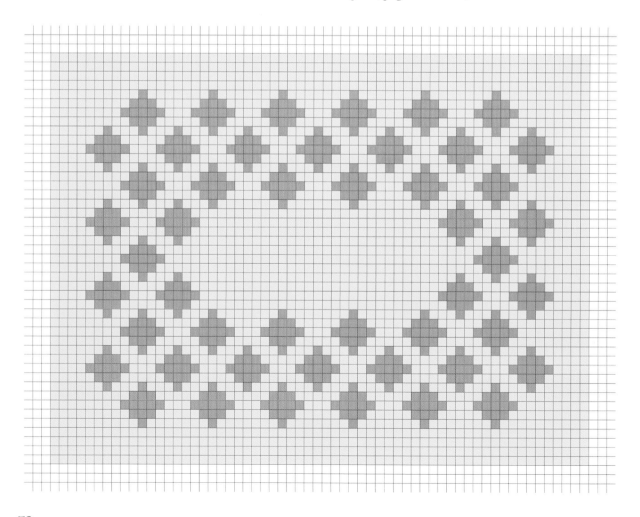

Finishing and Making Up

You will have spent many hours embroidering your rug, so it is worth taking the time to make the finishing as professional in appearance as possible. I find oversewing the edges makes a reliably neat finish and is not difficult to do. However, this is not essential (see below).

First remove your embroidery from the frame and, if necessary, pull it gently back into shape. If there is much distortion of the fabric you may need to block it (see Blocking, page 21). If you wish, you can lightly press the embroidery by placing it face down on a towel and pressing gently with a warm iron. When you are satisfied with the shape, trim the fabric, leaving a margin of about six holes from the embroidery. If necessary, use a proprietary product to stop fraying along the raw edges.

To oversew the edges (as for the Random Patch rug, pages 61–63), turn the edges under so that the next row of holes runs along the edges. Then, using at least three strands of the border-colour thread in your needle, begin oversewing, making sure you use the same holes as your last tent stitches occupied, and that your oversewing stitches all lie vertically through both layers of fabric. I find it easier to start a little way in from one of the corners and, when the next corner is reached, mitre the fabric and press down with my fingers, making the mitre join as neat as possible.

Continue oversewing, making sure you cover the corners well, and do not pull the thread too tightly, as this may allow the fabric to show through. When it is complete, apply a little fabric glue under the turned-down edges and press gently to stick it down.

Alternatively

Remove your embroidery from the frame and block and trim as above. Turn under all four edges and gently crease between your fingers and thumb, mitring the corners so that the last row of stitches forms the edge of the rug. (It is important to turn the fabric over sufficiently so that the unworked fabric cannot be seen from the right side.) Apply a little fabric glue and stick down one edge at a time.

Fringes

If you would like to add a fringe to your rug, you will need a piece of thin fabric, ideally in the same colour that your border has been worked. Cut two pieces of material, each a little longer than the ends of your rug and about ¾in (19mm) wide. Carefully fray this to whatever length you require by pulling out the cross threads one at a time. Using fabric glue, stick this to the underside of your rug and, when dry, trim the sides to the correct length. If the material is very thin you can put two layers together for a fuller look.

Chapter 5

Fire Screens

Fire screens are traditionally used to stand on a hearth when the fire is not alight, and they are often beautifully embroidered, adding decoration to the room.

I have included two designs for fire screens, both using traditional patchwork shapes. I have worked them on 30tpi to allow plenty of room for the design. But don't let that deter you, as they are both fairly quick to do, requiring no embroidery for the background. This is one of the advantages of using a fabric with a high number of threads per inch: as the holes are smaller, an unworked background does not look inappropriate.

DIFFICULTY
RATING

Snails Trail

Snails Trail is a fascinating patchwork shape, which in pieced patchwork is formed by an arrangement of squares and triangles. I know it is difficult to spot them in the pattern, but, honestly, they are there! I have confused the eye slightly by working this design in a random-dyed silk, but I think it makes the fire screen look rather special. You can, of course, embroider the design in a single-colour thread, or break it down into squares and triangles and embroider them in contrasting colours. Although the design does not take long to embroider, I have given it a difficulty rating of two, as it is worked on 30tpi and the placing of the pattern shapes is a little tricky, requiring some careful counting. It is worth the effort, though!

Materials
◆ 30tpi evenweave fabric
◆ Tapestry needle, size 28
◆ Fine random-dyed silk thread

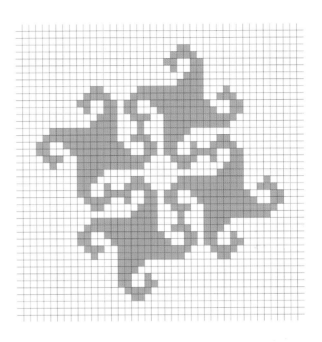

Stranded cotton

Not applicable for this pattern.

Embroidered design size	1⅛in (28mm) square
Stitch	tent
Stitch count	37 x 37
Stitch size	worked over every thread
Number of strands	1

Working method

Mount the fabric in a frame (I used a card frame for this piece, see pages 18–19), then begin by working the top curl of one of the four pattern shapes. Complete the shape, then move on to the next until all are worked. Do take care with the counting for this design – it doesn't look problematic but, I confess, the first time I embroidered it I misplaced one of the shapes. Finish and make up as described on page 80.

Variations

This design would also make a very pretty cushion or stool top. Alternatively, you could try embroidering it as a centre motif on a plain square rug on, say, 18tpi canvas. The embroidery size would then be approximately 2in (51mm) square, around which you could work a plain border (see Adapting Projects, pages 130–131).

DIFFICULTY RATING

Goose Chase

The pattern for this fire screen was created using the Goose Chase patchwork shape. Although the design is simple, I think it makes an attractive piece for the dolls' house. I have used just one colour, so it is very quick to work.

Materials

- ◆ 30tpi evenweave fabric
- ◆ Tapestry needle, size 28
- ◆ One colour of stranded cotton

Stranded cotton

▬ .... DMC 600

Embroidered design size .... ⅝ x 1⅜in (16 x 35mm)

Stitch .... tent

Stitch count .... 19 x 41

Stitch size .... worked over every thread

Number of strands 2

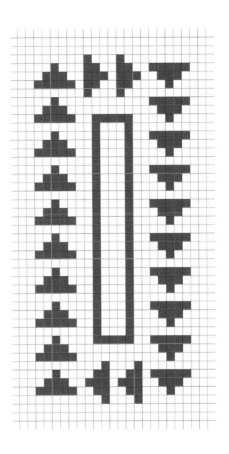

Working method

Mount the fabric in a frame (I used a card frame for this piece, see pages 18–19), then begin by working the rectangle in the centre. When it is complete, work the 'geese', which you should find easy to place in the correct position on your fabric by counting from the rectangle. Finish and make up as described on page 80.

Variations

Try using several different colours for a vibrant effect, or work the background in a contrasting colour. The size can be adapted to fit alternative shapes of fire screens, either by adding extra 'geese' along the top and bottom or reducing the number down the sides. (See Adapting Projects, pages 130–131.)

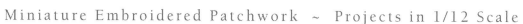
Finishing and Making Up

Remove your embroidery from the frame and, if you wish, press on the wrong side by laying it face down on a clean towel and pressing gently with a warm iron.

You may already have a fire screen frame that you wish to use, in which case cut a thin piece of card to fit it exactly and apply a small amount of fabric glue, scraping off any excess with a spare piece of card. Lay the fabric onto the card, while ensuring the embroidered part is centrally placed. (Sometimes it helps to hold it up to the light to check the position.) When you are happy, press gently to stick. Allow the glue to dry, then place a clean piece of paper or card onto a cutting board and lay the embroidery face down onto it. Using a metal ruler and very sharp craft knife, carefully cut away the excess fabric so that the fabric and card are exactly the same size. Apply a little glue to the fire screen and fix the embroidery to it.

To make your own fire screen, cut a thin piece of card and a matching piece of wood about ⅛in (3mm) thick to the size you require your finished frame to be. Stick your embroidery centrally to the card and, when dry, stick the card to the matching piece of wood. Paint or stain some moulded stripwood and when dry cut four pieces to fit onto the frame to form the raised edges, mitring the corners. Carefully stick to the embroidery to frame it, making sure the wood lies parallel and flush with the edges of the card. When dry, use a metal ruler and craft knife to cut away the excess fabric. Use two tiny pieces of wood (stained or painted to match your frame) to make the feet. (The small wooden blocks used for quoins on dolls' house walls, available from dolls' house suppliers, are ideal.) With a craft knife, cut a groove across each foot, the same width as the bottom of the frame and stand the frame in them. If necessary, apply a little wood glue to hold.

Chapter 5 ~ Fire Screens

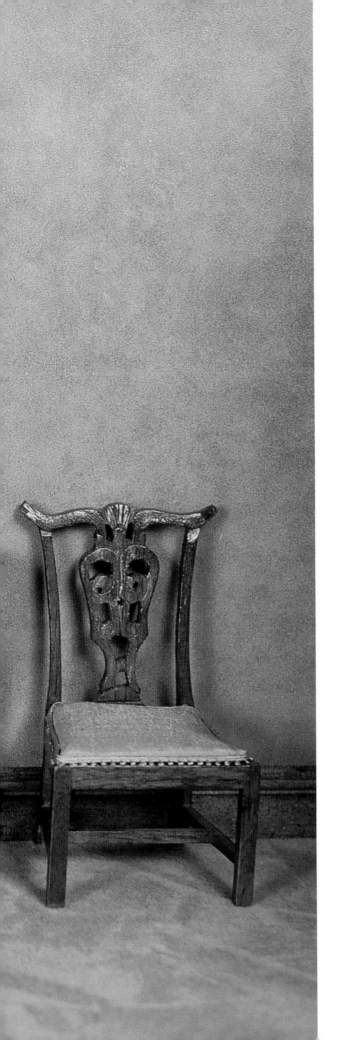

Chapter 6

Wall Hangings

Wall hangings provide an opportunity to show off a piece of treasured miniature embroidery to its best advantage in the dolls' house. They add colour, warmth and interest to any room, and are not difficult to make up as they do not need to be framed. The four wall hangings in this book are all quite different, requiring varying levels of expertise to make. I have included one suitable for the nursery, one which would suit a Tudor-style dolls' house, one designed as a sampler for patchwork shapes, and another which uses Florentine embroidery and looks wonderful against dark wood panelling. I am sure all will give you pleasure to work, and even more pleasure to display.

In addition to the wall hangings I have included a framed sampler to demonstrate the framing technique. If you wish, any of the wall hangings could be framed using the method described.

DIFFICULTY
RATING

Tudor

This wall hanging has a Tudor feel to it, which I think has more to do with the colours I have chosen than the patchwork shapes. I think it would look rather splendid in a dark, wood-panelled dining room or hall of a Tudor-style dolls' house.

The colours give the pattern definition, and the eye is deceived into thinking that each of the patchwork patterns is a regular shape. The design was interesting and enjoyable to work, but be careful with the counting to ensure correct placement of each pattern.

Materials
- 35tpi evenweave linen
- Embroidery needle, size 10
- Stranded cotton, as listed in key
- Spare fabric for loops

Stranded cotton

▇	.... DMC 814
▇	.... DMC 931
▇	.... DMC 3045

Design size ..2½ x 2¾in (64 x 70mm), excluding loops

Stitch ....tent

Stitch count...77 x 85

Stitch size ....worked over every thread

Number of strands 1

Working method

Mount the fabric in a frame (see pages 17–19), then begin by working the red cross at the top. Gradually work down the design, completing each patchwork shape before moving on to the next. Do not trail the threads from one shape to another, as they will almost certainly show through from the back. Finish each thread under the shape you are working and begin a new thread with the next shape. When all the shapes have been worked, start the outside border. I found it easiest to start in the middle of one side, where it is closest to the blue patchwork shape, as, that way, there is less counting and it is therefore easier to get the correct placing. When the outside border is complete, work the eight inside corner pieces. Finish and make up as described on page 99.

Variations

This design would make a lovely bedcover if both side borders were extended to the length you require. Make sure you extend by an even number of stitches, though, so that the pattern on the border still works.

DIFFICULTY
RATING

Florentine

I know this wall hanging owes more to the look of
Florentine (Bargello) stitch than it does to
patchwork, but I have seen full-size patchwork
quilts made by sewing together small rectangles of
different-colour fabrics to resemble a Florentine
pattern, and they always look very attractive.

Therefore, I decided to design a wall hanging that is
quite different from the others in this book. It is fairly
simple to work, once you get the pattern going. You
will find it is easiest to start somewhere near the
middle of the design and work one of the deeper-
coloured zigzags. The other zigzags follow on from
each other, so it is important to get the first row
exactly right.

Florentine patterns work well with five colours,
often three shades of one colour and two of another,
so you may wish to play around with graph paper and
coloured pencils to create your own design (see
Creating Your Own Designs, pages 132–133).

Materials
- 18tpi canvas
- Tapestry needle, size 22 or 24
- Stranded cotton, as listed in key
- Small piece of matching fabric for loops

Stranded cotton

▭	DMC 224
▭	DMC 372
▭	DMC 3685
▭	DMC 924
▭	DMC 832

Design size ..2½ x 3⅛in (64 x 79mm), excluding loops

Stitch ....tent

Stitch count..44 x 57

Stitch size ....worked over every thread

Number of strands 3

Working method

First mount the fabric in a frame (see pages 17–19). I suggest you then begin by working the central red zigzag right across the row, with three stitches for each small rectangle of colour. When you have completed this row it is worth looking at it closely to ensure that all the stitches are in the correct position, as the other rows follow its shape. When satisfied, work the zigzags above and below, each time finishing a row before going on to the next. When you are close to the top or bottom, make sure you don't get carried away and continue the zigzags further than they are meant to go. This is easily done, believe me! Refer to the chart for the last few rows, top and bottom. When you have completed the zigzags, work the two border rows. Finish and make up as described on page 99.

Variations

Try working this design on 27tpi for a lovely stool top with a finished size of approximately 1½ x 2in (38 x 51mm). Alternatively, increase the width and length of the zigzags to make a very fine-looking bedcover. (See Adapting Projects, pages 130–131.)

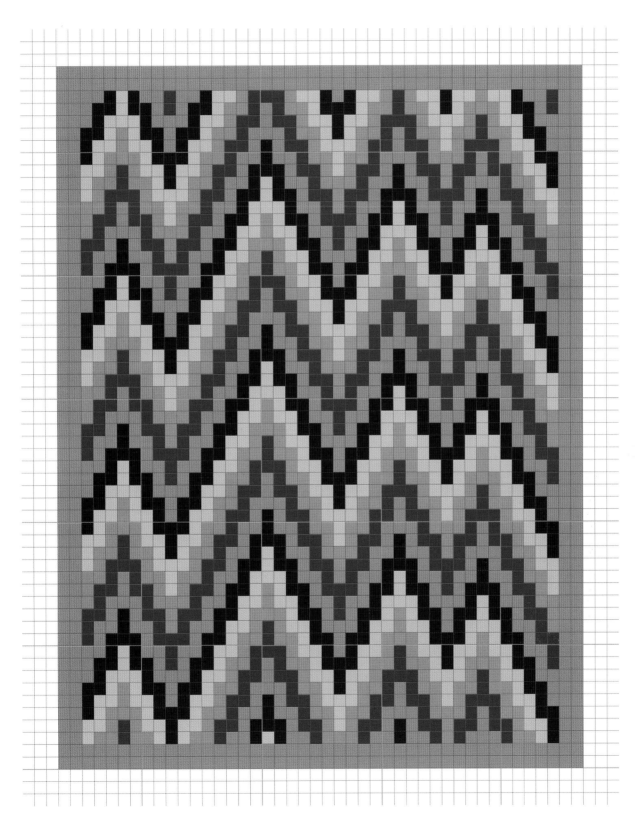

**DIFFICULTY
RATING**

Multi-Patch

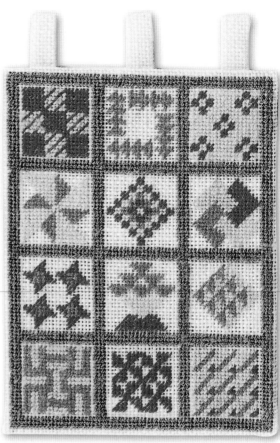

This is a striking wall hanging, which I thoroughly enjoyed designing and working. From top left to right the patchwork patterns are based on the following: Nine-Patch, Goose Chase, Nine-Patch, Windmill, Single-Patch, Card Trick, Friendship Star, Flower Basket, Birds in the Air, Rail Fence, Pinwheel and Roman Stripes.

I chose a limited palette of five colours, but if you wish to use a greater variety then this is an ideal pattern for using up any odd lengths of thread you may have. I hope you enjoy working this wall hanging, and I can almost guarantee you won't get bored with it, as there is no background to work and all the shapes are different.

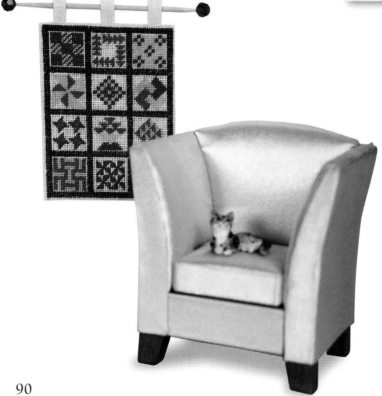

Materials
- 35tpi evenweave linen
- Embroidery needle, size 10
- Stranded cotton, as listed in key

90

Stranded cotton

■	DMC 304
▢	DMC 725
■	DMC 610
■	DMC 900
■	DMC 3819

Design size..............................2¼ x 2¾in (57 x 70mm)
excluding loops

Stitch ....tent

Stitch count...72 x 95

Stitch size ....worked over every thread

Number of strands 1

Working method

Mount the fabric in a frame (see pages 17–19), then begin by working the top left or right patch. When complete, work a length of the dividing line beside the patch, three stitches wide, as this will help with the placement of the next patch. Avoid trailing threads between one patch and another, as they will almost certainly show through from the back. Continue in this way, keeping the dividing lines going. When all the patches are complete, work the three border rows. Ensure all your stitches lie in the same direction. Finish and make up as described on page 99.

Variations

The patterns can be rearranged if desired. Alternatively, use fewer patterns and repeat them 'mirror fashion' from top to bottom. Any of these patches will make pretty cushions. Worked on 25tpi with a background colour extending by a few stitches either side of the pattern, you will have a cushion that is approximately 1in (25mm) square.

DIFFICULTY RATING

Little House on the Prairie

This was fun to work and could make an unusual wall hanging for a nursery. I have given it a difficulty rating of two, as the work is quite fine and correct placement of the houses is essential for a balanced look. It took about four hours for me to embroider, but I admit I kept changing the colour of the doors!

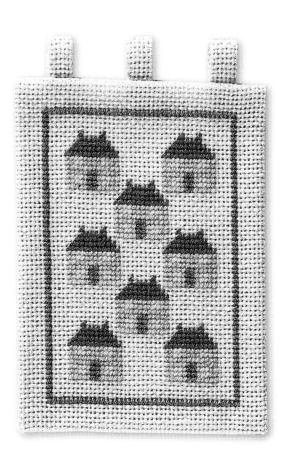

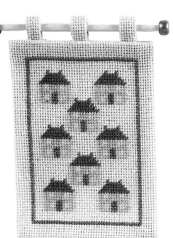

Materials

◆ 30tpi evenweave fabric
◆ Tapestry needle, size 28
◆ Stranded cotton, as listed in key
◆ Spare fabric for loops

Stranded cotton

▬	.... DMC 400
▬	.... DMC 731
▬	.... DMC 760
▬	.... DMC 726

Design size ..1¾ x 2¼in (44 x 57mm), excluding loops

Stitch ....tent

Stitch count..44 x 62

Stitch size ....worked over every thread

Number of strands 1

Working method

Mount the fabric in a frame (see pages 17–19), then start with one of the houses at the top left or right side, working the roof and walls first, then the windows and doors. Work the next house nearest to it (to help with the placing), and continue in this way until all the houses are complete. Finally, work the border row. Finish and make up as described on page 99.

Variations

If you have plenty of odd lengths of thread in your workbasket, try embroidering the houses in different colours. It will be especially suitable for a nursery if you include the three primary colours of red, blue and yellow. Working just one house on 18tpi fabric with a contrasting background colour extending on all sides about four threads beyond the house will make a nursery cushion of about 1in (25mm) square. (See Adapting Projects, pages 130–131.)

DIFFICULTY RATING

Framed Sampler

I know samplers usually include numbers and words, but I thought I would design this one with a mix of patchwork patterns. From the top down the patterns are: Roman Stripes, Single Patch, Windmill, Diamond Pattern, Hexagon, Diamond Pattern, Goose Chase and Roman Stripes. Although this sampler is worked on 35tpi linen, it is fairly quick to work, as there is no background stitching, and the variety of patterns means there is no boredom factor!

Materials
- ◆ 35tpi linen
- ◆ Embroidery needle, size 10
- ◆ Stranded cotton, as listed in key

96

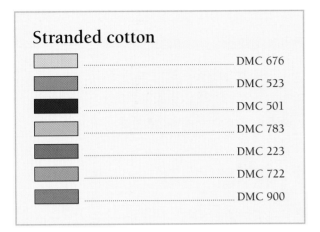

Stranded cotton

▭	DMC 676
▭	DMC 523
▭	DMC 501
▭	DMC 783
▭	DMC 223
▭	DMC 722
▭	DMC 900

Finished size,
including frame ....2 x 2¾in (51 x 70mm)

Stitch ....tent

Stitch count.......................................47 x 72

Stitch size ....worked over every thread

Number of strands 1

Working method

Mount the fabric in a frame (see pages 17–19), then start at the top left or right corner, completing each pattern in the row before progressing to the next. Work the border with a single stitch all around.

Variations

Try embroidering your own selection of patchwork patterns, using patchwork books and magazines for inspiration, and create a unique sampler. Aim for a balance of colour and shapes.

To frame the sampler

You can purchase many sizes of 1/12 scale ready-made frames from miniatures shops, or you may already have one you can use. However, if you would like to make your own, the method Pamela Warner uses in her book *Miniature Embroidery for the Victorian Dolls' House* by GMC Publications works particularly well.

Materials
◆ Thin card
◆ Fabric glue
◆ 1/12 scale narrow moulding

Remove your embroidery from the frame and, if necessary, pull it gently to shape. If your embroidery has become badly distorted, you may need to block it (see Blocking, page 21). If you wish, the embroidery can be lightly pressed by placing it face down on a clean towel and pressing gently with a warm iron. Next, cut a thin piece of card that is approximately 2 x 2¾in (51 x 70mm) and put a very thin layer of glue on it, removing all excess immediately with a spare piece of card. (There should only be enough left on the card to make it feel slightly sticky, otherwise you risk the glue leaving a mark on the embroidery.) Lay the embroidery onto the glue, making sure it is straight, then press very gently to fix. Leave to dry. Stain or paint your wooden moulding, then, using a mitre saw and wood glue, make up the frame to fit the size of the card. When the glue has set, place your frame over the embroidery and stick it in place. Leave to dry. Finally, with a very sharp craft knife, carefully cut away the excess fabric.

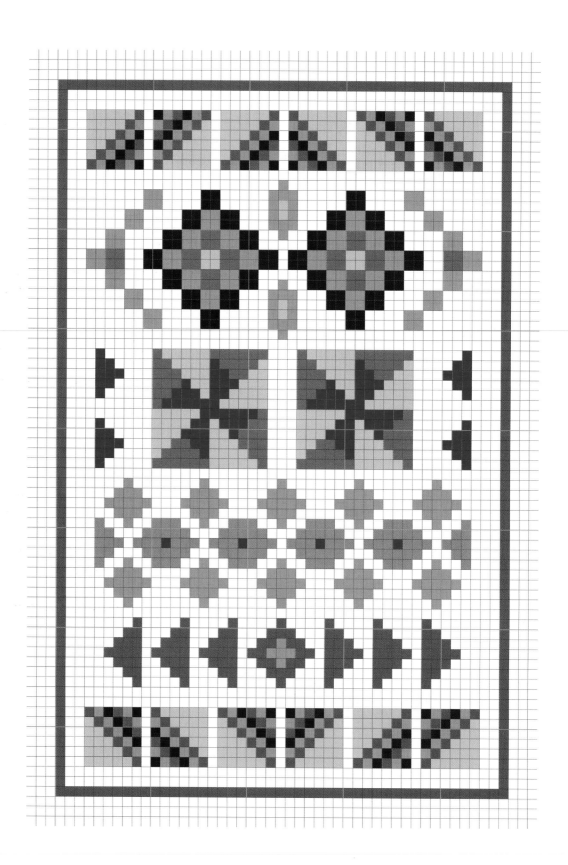

Finishing and Making Up

Making up wall hangings is blissfully simple but, as always, care should be taken to get the finish as professional as possible with neat square corners.

Firstly, remove your embroidery from the frame and, if necessary, pull it gently back into shape. If the fabric is badly distorted, you may wish to block it (see Blocking, page 21). Press lightly on the wrong side by placing it face down and pressing gently with a warm iron, if desired.

Tudor, Little House on the Prairie and Multi-Patch

When you are satisfied with the shape of your embroidery, fold the excess fabric over, fairly close to the embroidery. (The amount of unworked fabric you leave showing on the front is entirely up to you, depending on the finished size you wish your wall hanging to be). Crease these folds lightly between your fingers and thumb, then carefully cut away the excess fabric so that the turned-over edges are approximately ¼in (6mm) wide. Apply a small amount of fabric glue along the back of the side edges of the embroidery and carefully stick down. When dry, fold over and stick the top and bottom edges. By just folding the edges in you will find you can achieve very neat corners without mitring them. Leave to dry. In the meantime, cut a length of the spare embroidery fabric about ⅝in (16mm) wide and about 4in (102mm) long. Place a thin line of fabric glue down the centre and fold over one long side so that it is approximately two thirds in, then immediately fold the other side over until it is just short of the opposite edge. Press together with your fingers.(Take care that your folds are with the straight grain of the fabric.) When dry, cut three short lengths and fold each in half lengthways with the join on the inside and space evenly along the back at the top edge, leaving just enough loop showing above the embroidery to take a piece of narrow doweling. Apply a small amount of glue on the bottom of each loop and stick down along the back edge.

NB: As a rule, the larger the wall hanging the larger the loops should be in order to look balanced.

When dry, push a small piece of doweling through the loops, allowing it to extend slightly beyond the wall hanging. Push two hooks into your dolls' house wall and rest the doweling on them. Alternatively, drill a tiny hole at either end of the doweling and thread a fine piece of cord through them, knotting each end. Use the cord to hang the wall hanging from a single hook.

Florentine

Proceed as above but turn the excess fabric under until the last row of embroidery stitches forms the edges. Continue as above but make the loops from a piece of fine matching material, rather than the 18tpi embroidery fabric, as this would look heavy and unsightly.

Chapter 7

Bedcovers

O ne of the most important pieces of furniture in a dolls' house bedroom is, of course, the bed, and your choice of bedcoverings can hugely influence the look of the room. You may want a cheerful look, a romantic look, a masculine or feminine look, or a look that is just plain fun. With this in mind, I have designed five very different bedcovers to enhance your beds, introducing Rhodes stitch for two of them. (Be warned: Rhodes stitch is addictive, and you may find you end up with more items in your dolls' house worked in this stitch than you intended!) They all look effective laid on top of floor-length, thin bed covers, or sheets and blankets, and they can be backed and padded with a soft fabric to give the look of a quilt. I hope you will enjoy working them as much I have.

DIFFICULTY RATING

Midnight

The striking mauves and dark blues within this bedcover conjured up images of the midnight sky, hence the name I have given it. I have taken my inspiration for this vibrant design from the simple patchwork method of joining together squares of various patterned fabrics to form a bedcover. I have used nine colours and randomly repeated the designs, which might make the project look a little daunting. However, each patchwork square is only eleven stitches across and down, and if you concentrate on just one square at a time, with short lengths of thread in your needle, you can't go wrong – honestly!

Materials
- ◆ 27tpi evenweave fabric
- ◆ Tapestry needle, size 26 or 28
- ◆ Stranded cotton, as listed in key

Stranded cotton

▬	DMC 333
▬	DMC 3811
▬	DMC 553
▬	DMC 3810
▬	DMC 554
▬	DMC 718
▬	DMC 793
▬	DMC 336
▬	DMC 316

Design size............................3½ x 4½in (89 x 114mm)

Stitch ....tent

Stitch count...96 x 118

Stitch size ....worked over every thread

Number of strands 2

Working method

Mount your fabric in a frame (see pages 17–19), then begin at the top left or right corner, working one patchwork square at a time. Work across and down until all the squares are complete, then work the four border rows. Ensure all your stitches lie in the same direction. By always working the patchwork square next to the one you have just completed (rather than jumping about to suit the thread in your needle) you will have very little counting to do and you will not risk misplacing a square. Finish and make up as described on page 117.

Variations

Just four of the patches from this pattern can be worked as a cushion. Alternatively, try designing some patterns of your own, using graph paper and coloured pencils. You can then create your own unique bedcover and matching cushions. (See Adapting Projects, pages 130–131.)

DIFFICULTY
RATING

Windmill

I have repeated the easily recognized Windmill pattern for this bedcover using just three colours. I like the slight optical illusion created by the eye picking up either the red or pink windmills. The design is made up entirely of three different-size triangles, repeated throughout to form a complex-looking pattern. However, because of the repetitious nature of the design, you will soon work each patch from memory without needing to keep looking at the pattern.

I have given it a difficulty rating of three, more because of the length of time it takes to embroider than its complexity – it took me about thirty hours. However, it was fun to work, with very little counting.

Materials
- ◆ 27tpi evenweave fabric
- ◆ Tapestry needle, size 26 or 28
- ◆ Stranded cotton, as listed in key

Stranded cotton

▬	.... DMC 718
▬	.... DMC 778
▬	.... DMC 677

Design size .... 3¼ x 4in (84 x 100mm)

Stitch .... tent

Stitch count .... 86 x 106

Stitch size .... worked over every thread

Number of strands 2

Working method

Mount your fabric in a frame (see pages 17–19), then begin by embroidering the red triangle at the top left or right corner. Work the pink patches around it and then the yellow. Try to finish off the threads under the back of the stitches that are in the same colour. Continue along the row, working one square at a time, then the remaining rows. Finally, work the three border rows. Ensure all your stitches lie in the same direction. Finish and make up as described on page 117.

Variations

You may like to use a greater variety of colours for the windmills, giving a completely different look to the pattern. Use graph paper and coloured pencils to get an idea of how it will appear, or work a small sample. This pattern can also be adapted to a cushion by using just four of the patches with a three-row border. On 35tpi the finished size will be approximately 1¼in (31mm) square, and on 27tpi approximately 1¾in (44mm) square. (See Adapting Projects, pages 130–131.)

**DIFFICULTY
RATING**

Suffolk Puffs I

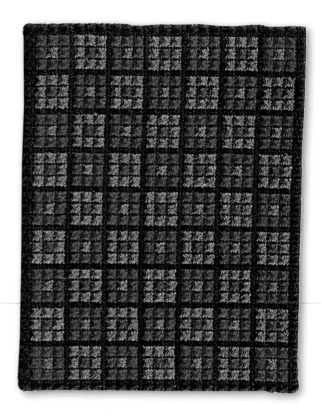

Suffolk Puffs is a form of pieced patchwork comprising small fabric circles that have running stitches around the edges. These stitches are pulled to form tiny gathered puffs, which are then sewn together to make bed and cot covers. The effect is delicate and textural, and I have tried to simulate this form of patchwork by embroidering this bedcover in Rhodes stitch. The very nature of the stitch ensures a little raised 'puff', giving an interesting surface pattern. It is worth spending a little time practising the stitch (see page 16) on a spare piece of fabric. Once mastered, I think you will find working this stitch quite therapeutic.

The bedcover is relatively quick to work, as the Rhodes stitch covers three threads of the fabric at a time. I have given it a difficulty rating of three, as it is necessary to take care with the placement of the stitches and the rows of tent stitches in between, but once you start forming the pattern you should find you are able to work the entire bedcover without referring to the chart.

Materials
- 24tpi evenweave fabric
- Tapestry needle, size 26 or 28
- Stranded cotton, as listed in key

Stranded cotton

■	DMC 958
■	DMC 718
■	DMC 550

Design size ....3 x 4in (76 x 102mm)

Stitch ....Rhodes, with single row of tent

Stitch count...75 x 95

Stitch size ...Rhodes over 3 threads, tent over 1 thread

Number of strands ....2 for Rhodes, 3 for tent

Working method

The embroidery is worked in Rhodes stitch with a single row of tent stitch between each patchwork square. First mount your fabric in a frame (see pages 17–19) and then work the nine Rhodes stitches at the top left or right corner. I recommend you work the rows of single tent stitch as you go, to ensure you don't forget to leave space for them and also to help with the counting. Work along the first row, completing each 'patch' as you go, then begin the second, and continue until all the patches are complete. Work one row of Rhodes stitch around the edges, remembering to continue the lines of tent stitch as before. Ensure you work each Rhodes stitch the same way, so that they look uniform. Finish and make up as described on page 117.

Variations

Try working either four or nine of the patches to make matching cushions, or work four patches across and three down for a lovely stool top. (See Adapting Projects, pages 130–131.)

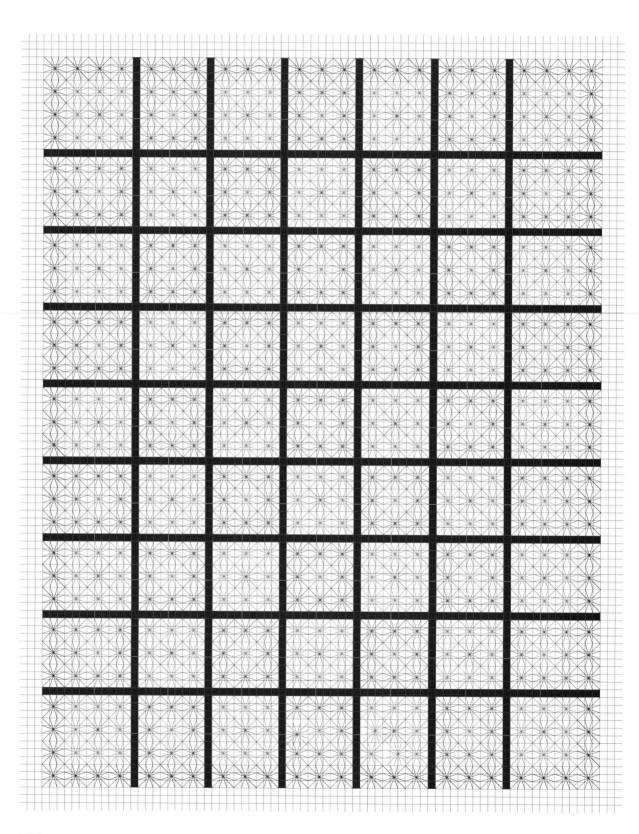

DIFFICULTY RATING

Suffolk Puffs II

For this second 'Suffolk Puffs' bedcover I have chosen a bold, geometric pattern, which would look lovely in a bright, fresh room setting. I have used a limited number of colours, and varied the order of them within the patchwork squares, so that 'diamond' shapes are formed. If Rhodes stitch is new to you, I recommend you spend a little time practising it on a spare piece of fabric (see page 16). As with the previous design, I have given it a difficulty rating of three, but don't be deterred by this, as the Rhodes stitch covers three threads of fabric at a time, so, once mastered, your bedcover will quickly increase in size.

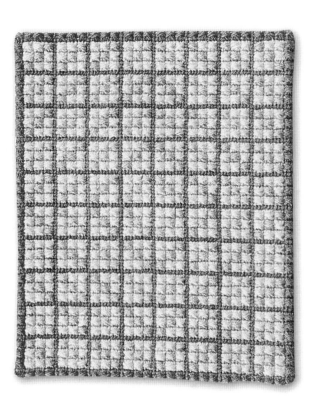

Materials
- ◆ 27tpi evenweave fabric
- ◆ Tapestry needle, size 26 or 28
- ◆ Stranded cotton, as listed in key

Stranded cotton

▬	.... DMC 350
▬	.... DMC 369
▭	.... DMC 445

Design size .... 3 x 3¾in (76 x 95mm)

Stitch .... Rhodes, with single row of tent

Stitch count .... 85 x 105

Stitch size .... worked over 3 threads (Rhodes) and over 1 thread (tent)

Number of strands 2

Working method

The embroidery is worked in Rhodes stitch, with a single row of tent stitch between each patchwork square. Mount your fabric in a frame (see pages 17–19), then begin by working the nine Rhodes stitches at the top left or right corner. I recommend you work the rows of single tent stitch as you go, to ensure you don't forget to leave space for them and to help with the counting. Work along the first row of patchwork squares, then begin the second. Continue until all the patches are complete, carefully watching the placement of colours so that your diamond shapes are formed. Ensure you work each Rhodes stitch in the same way so that they all look uniform. Finish and make up as described on page 117.

Variations

Try your own colour combinations, maybe using just two colours for the Rhodes stitches. A bedcover would look very pretty worked in alternate patches (nine Rhodes stitches in each) of, say, pale and dark blues. Use a different shade of blue for the rows of tent stitch and the borders.

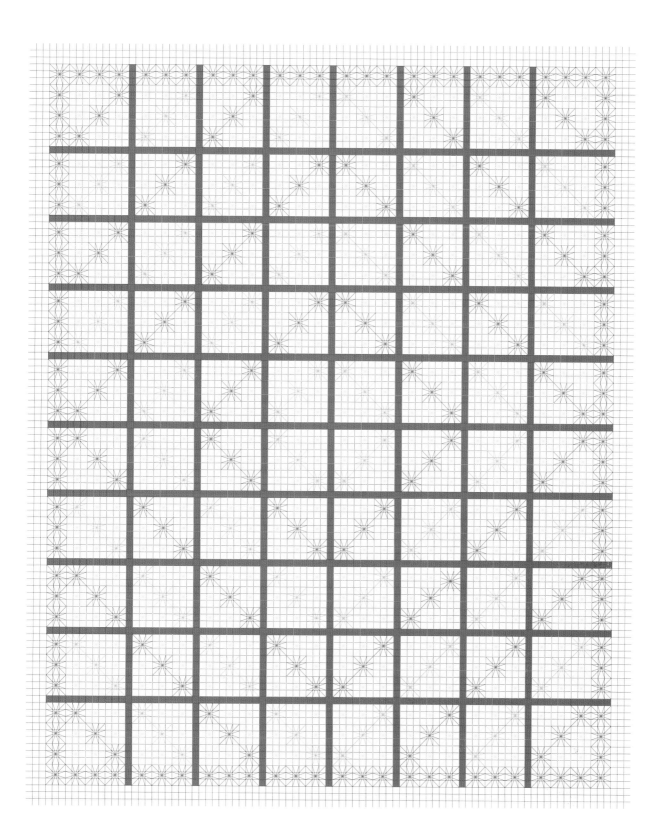

**DIFFICULTY
RATING**

Multi-Patch

I wanted to embroider a bedcover in deep colours suitable for a boy's bedroom, and I decided to design this one with a multi-patch effect. Although I have used just three colours, the effect is of quite an intricate pattern, with the dividing lines giving it some uniformity. Multi-patch designs are interesting to work, as there is very little risk of boredom – quite the opposite in fact, as I find when I am working them I keep wanting to do just one more patch to see how it looks!

Materials
- 25tpi evenweave fabric
- Tapestry needle, size 26 or 28
- Stranded cotton, as listed in key

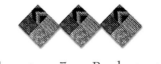

Stranded cotton

██	DMC 3685
██	DMC 523
██	DMC 501

Design size.............................1⅞ x 3¼in (47 x 82mm)

Stitch ....tent

Stitch count....................................46 x 79

Stitch size ....worked over every thread

Number of strands 2

Working method

Mount your fabric in a frame (see pages 17–19), then begin by embroidering the patch at the top left or right corner. I recommend you work the red dividing lines as you go, so that you don't forget to leave space for them; you will find this also helps with the counting. Continue working the squares along and down. When complete, work the two border rows. Ensure all your stitches lie in the same direction. Finish and make up as described on page 117.

Variations

This pattern will adapt well to a rug by working on 18tpi canvas. The finished size will be approximately 2½ x 4½in (64 x 114mm). You could also make cushions to match the bedcover by working on 25tpi and using either four or nine of the patches with a small border. (See Adapting Projects, pages 130–131.)

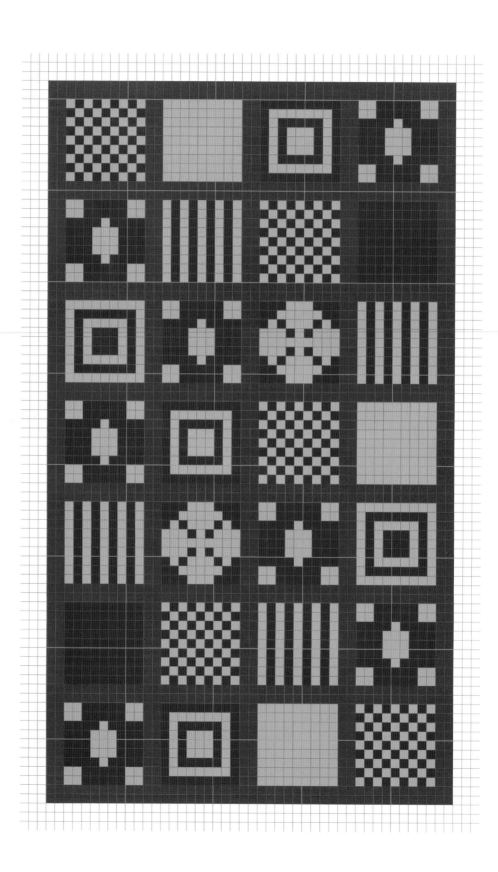

Finishing and Making Up

There are various ways of finishing bedcovers. The following are methods I have used.

Midnight and Windmill

For these bedcovers I have oversewn the edges. First remove your embroidery from the frame. If there is much distortion of the fabric, carefully block it (see Blocking, page 21). Now proceed as for Finishing and Making Up for the Random-Patch rug (see pages 61–63). You may prefer just to turn the edges under so that the last row of embroidery forms the edging, as in the bedcovers below.

Multi-Patch

Remove your embroidery from the frame and, if it has become distorted, carefully block it (see Blocking, page 21). Next, trim the fabric, leaving a six-hole margin from the embroidery, and turn under all four edges, mitring the corners, so that the last row of stitches forms the edge of the bedcover. Apply a little fabric glue under the turned-back edges and press down gently.

Suffolk Puffs I & II

You should find you have little or no distortion of the fabric with this stitch. I have finished them in the same way as for the Multi-Patch bedcover by trimming the fabric to about six holes from the embroidery and then turning the edges under, gluing and pressing down gently.

Backing

If you wish, you can back the bedcovers with a silky fabric. To do this, carefully cut a piece of matching fabric the same size as the finished bedcover and press under about ⅛in (3mm) all around. Place the fabric centrally on the back of your cover (WRONG sides together) and, with a fine sewing needle and sewing thread, hem the two together. Try to keep your stitches as small as possible. For a 'plumper' look, cut two pieces of a soft cotton fabric a little smaller than your lining material (after turning under the edges) and place between the bedcover and lining.

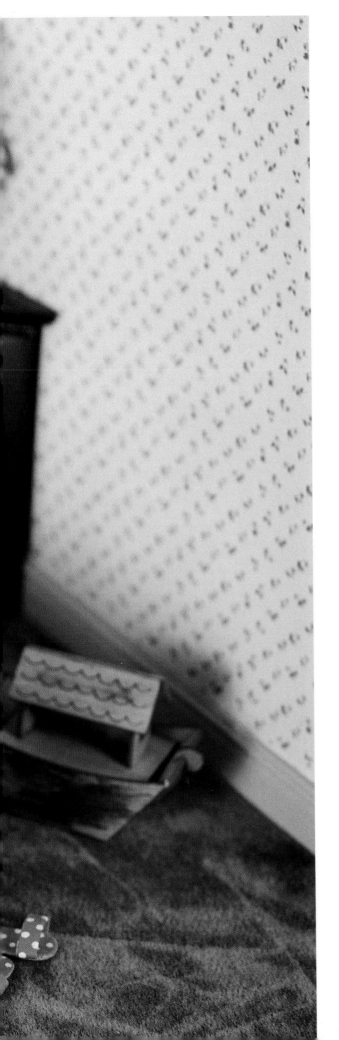

Chapter 8

Chests

Many years ago, chests were used to transport a person's belongings, either on a long journey or when fleeing from invasion. Today, they form a decorative and useful addition to many people's homes, often positioned at the foot of a bed, placed by a window as occasional seating or used by children to store their toys. I have designed three very different chest tops, each finished with a different trimming, which I hope you will enjoy embroidering. Full details of how to attach your embroidery to a chest are given at the end of the chapter.

**DIFFICULTY
RATING**

Windmill

The popular windmill patchwork shape on this chest is made up of triangles, and I have placed them closely together to form a highly patterned look. I have chosen colours from opposite sides of the colour wheel that complement each other yet give a vibrant effect, and then used a gentle background colour. I think this chest would look splendid in a richly wallpapered bedroom in the dolls' house, perhaps with matching red velvet drapes.

Materials
- 28tpi evenweave linen
- Tapestry needle, size 26 or 28
- Stranded cotton, as listed in key

Stranded cotton

(dark)	DMC 501
(dark)	DMC 304
(light)	DMC 676

Design size	3½ x 1¾in (89 x 44mm)
Stitch	tent
Stitch count	99 x 50
Stitch size	worked over every thread
Number of strands	2

Working method

Mount the fabric in a frame (see pages 17–19), then begin by embroidering the top left or right windmill. Finish each windmill before moving on to the one beside it, as you are then less likely to misplace them. It is helpful to have two needles threaded at the same time, one with green, the other with red. When you have completed all the windmills, work the background, ensuring throughout that your stitches lie in the same direction. Finish and make up as described on page 128.

Variations

The stitch count for this design will fit many commercially available 1/12 scale wooden chests. However, if you should need to extend it, simply work a few more rows in the background colour until your embroidery fits the top of the chest. If the chest is slightly smaller, either work one or two less border rows, or consider using a fabric with a higher number of threads to the inch. Matching cushions are easily made by working one windmill on 22tpi fabric with the background colour extending about four rows on all sides of it. This will give you a cushion that is approximately 1in (25mm) square. (See Adapting Projects, pages 130–131.)

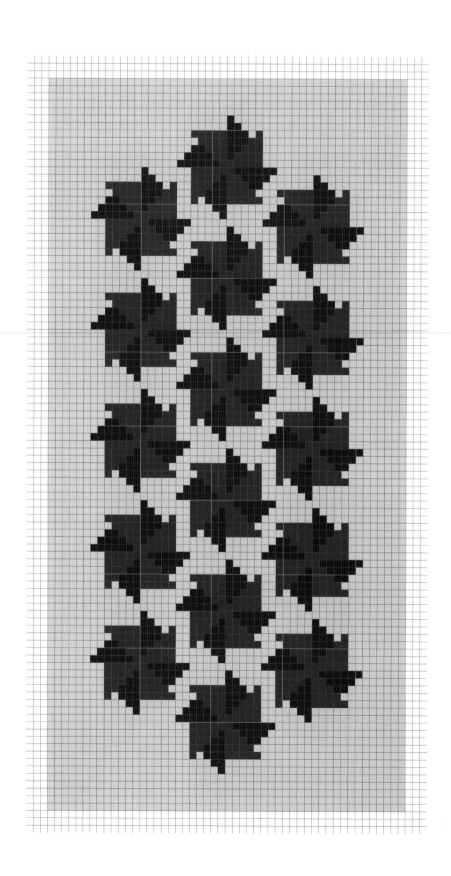

DIFFICULTY
RATING

Diamond Pattern

I have taken the basic diamond shape for this chest and embroidered three rows of diamonds in two different random-dyed colours, with a random-dyed yellow for the background. To avoid confusing the eye, I have divided each diamond with a solid pink line, and continued the pink for the borders. This pretty chest would look very attractive at the foot of a delicately dressed bed, and would also make a lovely toy box for a little girl.

Materials
- 25tpi evenweave fabric
- Tapestry needle, size 24 or 26
- Random-dyed DMC stranded cotton, colours 107, 108 and 124
  Pink DMC, colour 3733

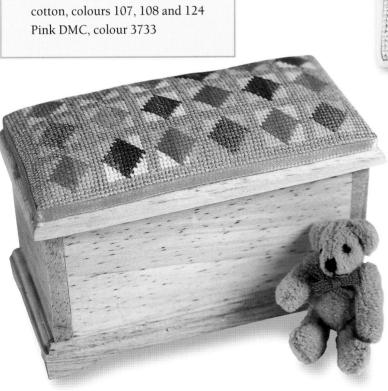

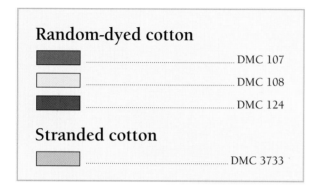

Random-dyed cotton

�	.... DMC 107
	.... DMC 108
	.... DMC 124

Stranded cotton

	.... DMC 3733

Design size..............................3¾ x 1⅞in (95 x 47mm)

Stitch ....tent

Stitch count...89 x 45

Stitch size ....worked over every thread

Number of strands 2

Working method

When using random-dyed threads, you will probably find that each of the colour variations along the length of the skein is several inches long, as it will not have been dyed for miniature embroidery. This means that you could work quite a large area in miniature and not notice any colour variation. To avoid this happening, be selective in the length of thread you use, and each time you re-thread your needle cut a short length where there is some variation that pleases you. As in this case, where you require two strands in your needle, try to ensure the colours of each strand are similar, otherwise you will have a 'spotted' effect, rather than graduations of colour.

First mount your fabric in a frame (see pages 17–19), then begin by embroidering the diamond in the top left or right corner of the chart. Before moving on to the next diamond, I suggest you work a little of the pink line that divides the diamonds, as this will help with the placing. Continue in this way, until you have completed all the diamonds and dividing lines. Finally, work the border rows. Finish and make up as described on page 128.

Variations

If necessary, this design can be enlarged to fit a chest you already own by simply extending the number of border rows all around. If the embroidered top is going to be too large for the chest, consider using a fabric with a higher number of threads per inch. (See Adapting Projects, pages 130–131.)

DIFFICULTY
RATING

Octagonal Pattern

Sometimes I like the challenge of working on a fabric with a fairly high count, so I decided to design this chest top for 35tpi fabric. It is a delicate pattern, for which I have used fairly subdued colours, but there are many other colour combinations that you could try to suit your own dolls' house decor. How about using colours from opposite sides of the colour wheel that complement each other, or three colours equal distance apart to give a vibrant effect? Try your chosen colours on graph paper, using coloured pencils to see how you like them, or work a small sample piece. This chest does not take long to embroider, as there is no background to work, but be careful with the counting to ensure that all parts of the pattern are correctly placed. I have chosen an ecru linen on which to embroider, but you may like to choose a more brightly coloured fabric and then alter the colour threads you use to contrast with it. Either way, I hope you enjoy working this little chest top.

Materials
- ◆ 35tpi evenweave fabric
- ◆ Embroidery needle, size 10
- ◆ Stranded cotton, as listed in key

Stranded cotton

(dark)	DMC 632
(light)	DMC 783
(medium)	DMC 900

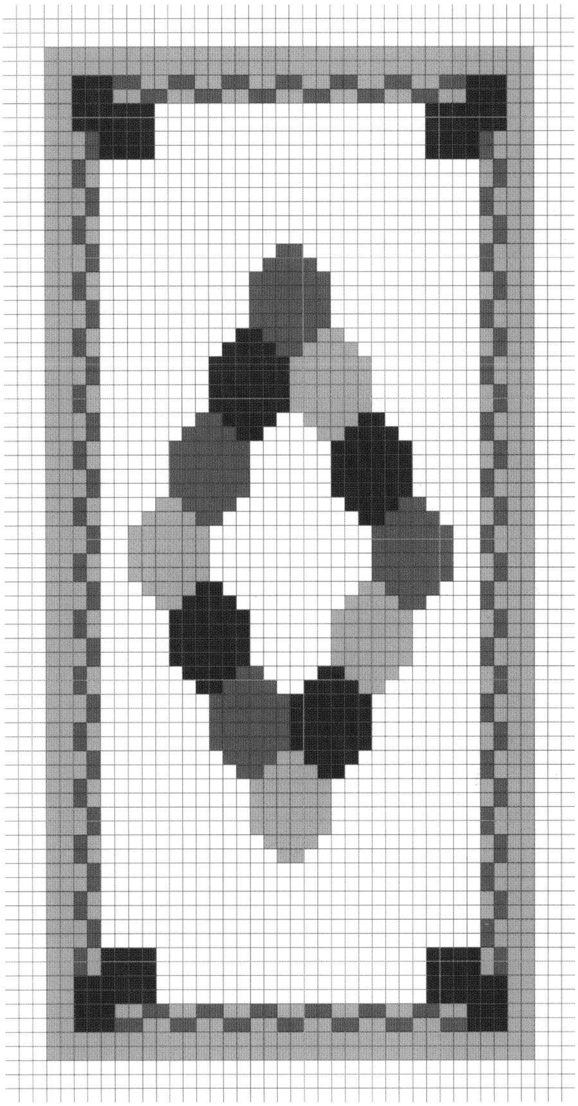

Design size	2 x 1in (51 x 25mm)
Stitch	tent
Stitch count	72 x 36
Stitch size	worked over every thread
Number of strands	1

Working method

Mount the fabric in a frame (see pages 17–19), then begin by stitching the octagons in the centre. Do not trail your thread between the octagons, as this will show through from the back. Instead, finish each octagon by running your needle under the back of the last few stitches you have worked in that colour. Re-thread your needle for the next octagon. When all the octagons are worked, embroider the border, then, finally, the brown areas at each corner. Finish and make up as described on page 128.

Variations

This pattern can be worked on a lower count fabric. If you use 24tpi, the embroidered area will measure approximately 3 x 1½in (76 x 38mm), which would be ideal for a window seat or long stool. (See Adapting Projects, pages 130–131.)

Finishing and Making Up

Hopefully, your finished embroidery will fit your chest top, either by using the same fabric and stitch count as I have, or by adapting the pattern or fabric (see Adapting Projects, pages 130–131). Ideally, the embroidery should be slightly larger all around than the chest top to allow for the padding.

First remove your embroidery from the frame and, if necessary, pull it gently into shape. If your embroidery is badly distorted, you may need to block it (see Blocking, page 21). If you wish, the embroidery can be lightly pressed by placing face down on a clean towel and pressing gently with a warm iron. When you are satisfied with the shape, trim the excess fabric, leaving a margin of about six holes from the embroidery. Cut a piece of thin card the same size as your chest top (no larger) and place a thin piece of foam or some wadding on top. Use dabs of glue to stick this to the card. Lay your embroidery on top, making sure it is positioned centrally, and fold under one long side so that the embroidery is at the edge of the card. Stick down with fabric glue. Leave to dry, then fold under the opposite side and stick down, pulling gently to get a nice, rounded shape. When dry, fold and stick both ends, turning the corners under as neatly and flat as possible. When all is dry, stick to the top of your chest. Finish by applying a tiny amount of fabric glue to one edge at a time and attach your chosen trimming, which will hide the join between the chest and embroidery. It is best to start the trimming half way along the back, and where the trimming meets, allow a tiny overlap.

Chapter 9

Adapting Projects

All the designs in this book can be adapted to suit your needs. For instance, if you wish to make your finished embroidery a different size, consider changing the fabric. If you use a fabric with a higher number of threads to the inch (tpi) your embroidery will work out smaller, and if you use a fabric with a smaller number of threads to the inch it will work out larger. Alternatively, you may be able to add to the number of background or border rows to make the item larger, or reduce the background and maybe do without a border for a smaller item.

Always remember, when you are changing the fabric count (number of threads to the inch) you may also need to change your needle size and the number of thread strands in your needle. You only need enough strands to cover the fabric; if you use more than necessary your embroidery will appear bulky and could look out of scale.

You may wish to change the overall colour scheme (see Colour Guidelines, pages 22–23), or use just part of a pattern to make a different item, such as a cushion from part of a bedcover pattern. All the designs consist of either rectangles or squares, and if you think of them in this way you are more likely to be able to see ways of adapting them.

Calculating size

To be able to adapt the designs you first need to know how to calculate what size your finished embroidery will be. If you are using part of a pattern from one of the designs in this book, use the chart to count how many stitches (squares) there are across and down,

remembering to include any background or borders you may like to have. Let us say the stitch count is 36 x 45. This means you will need 36 threads of fabric across and 45 threads of fabric down to complete the design (plus turnings). You now need to divide these numbers by the number of threads to the inch on your chosen fabric. If you choose 18tpi, then 36 divided by 18 = 2 (so your embroidery will be 2in (51mm) across, and 45 divided by 18 = 2.5 (so your embroidery will be 2½in (64mm) down. This would be a little large for a cushion, for instance, so you may choose to use a 24tpi fabric instead. Again, to calculate the finished size of the embroidery, 36 divided by 24 = 1.5 (so your embroidery will be 1½in (38mm) across, and 45 divided by 24 = 1.875 (so your embroidery will be approximately 2in (51mm) down – a more appropriate size for a cushion.

Creating a rug from part of a chart in this book

You can take part of a design from this book and use it as the central pattern for a rug. Decide what size you would like the rug to be and which fabric count you will be using. For example, say you would like your rug to be 5 x 3½in (127 x 89mm) and you are using 24tpi fabric. Calculate how many stitches your rug will have across and down by multiplying the number of inches by the number of threads to the inch of your fabric: 5 x 24in = 120, and 3½ x 24in = 84, so your rug will have a total stitch count of 120 x 84. Provided the design you wish to copy has no more stitches than this, you can now copy it straight from the book. To do this,

use graph paper, a pencil and ruler, and draw out a rectangle with 120 squares across and 84 down. Then, using coloured pencils, colour in the squares where you want the pattern to be, copying from the chart and making sure you place it centrally. You will now have a fairly good idea of the proportions, and whether or not you would like (or indeed there is room) for a border.

Repeating pattern shapes

To increase a cushion design by repeating it to make, for example, a bedcover, first decide on what size you would like your bedcover to be. For instance, you may like it to be approximately 3 x 4½in (76 x 114mm) and the cushion pattern is approximately 1½in (38mm) square, as with the Blue and Cream Nine-Patch cushion on pages 28–29. You will need to divide 3 by 1½, which equals 2 (the number of pattern repeats across) and 4½ by 1½, which equals 3 (the number of pattern repeats down). In the case of the blue and cream cushion, you may not want to repeat the three-row border for each pattern repeat, which will reduce the overall size slightly.

If you wish to cover a long stool or window seat, try repeating a cushion motif until the design is the required size. The Eight-Triangle cushion design would work particularly well for this. Map out your repeated design on graph paper (copying it from the chart) to make sure you like the way it looks before starting to embroider. In this case, I suggest the triangle patterns need to be no more than three threads of fabric apart. If repeated three times, you would have a stitch count of 78 across (3 for the edging, 22 for the pattern, 3 in

between, 22 for the pattern, 3 in between, 22 for the pattern and another 3 for the edging) plus the original 28 down. Worked on 27tpi fabric this will mean 78 divided by 27 = just under 3 x 1in (76 x 25mm), which would be ideal for a window seat. Worked on 35tpi fabric the figures are: 78 divided by 35 = 2¼ x just under 1in (approximately 57mm x 25mm) – perfect for a stool top.

Adapting a cushion to fit a stool top

You will probably be able to do this just by altering the number of background colour rows until the embroidery fits the top of your stool. In which case, always ensure the pattern remains central. Alternatively, consider using a fabric with a different number of threads to the inch.

Adapting a bedcover design for a rug

It may be possible just to alter the number of threads per inch of the fabric you use to create the size of rug you would like. For example, the Multi-Patch bedcover is worked on 25tpi with a stitch count of 79 x 46, giving an overall size of approximately 3¼ x 1⅞in (82 x 47mm). If you work the same design on 18tpi canvas, your finished size will be approximately 4½ x 2½in (114 x 64mm), i.e. 79 divided by 18 = approximately 4.5, and 46 divided by 18 = approximately 2.5. The Windmill bedcover could be used as it is for a rug, or you could extend the border colour by several rows all around to make it a little larger.

Chapter 10

Creating Designs

Miniature embroidery is enjoyable, creative, and addictive, so what more could one ask for? Well, add to that the fun and satisfaction that can be gained from creating your own designs and you really will be a happy person!

When I suggest this to my students the response I hear most often is that they couldn't possibly design their own pattern, and wouldn't even dare to try. However, it really is very simple, and perhaps the best advice I can give is to start with a fairly straightforward shape and repeat it, perhaps 'mirror fashion', until a design appears. Use pencils to colour in squares on graph paper (each square will represent one stitch), and when you are satisfied with the result perhaps put a plain border around it. You will then have your first unique design ready to work as a cushion, or perhaps a rug.

Colour plays an enormous part in designing, so for advice refer to Colour Guidelines, pages 22–23.

For designing you will need:
◆ Graph paper
◆ Pencil
◆ Eraser
◆ Coloured pencils

To start designing

Decide on the finished size of item you are to design and what count of fabric you are happy with. 18, 22 and 24tpi fabrics are suitable for carpets, and 24–40tpi work well for items such as cushions. Calculate the number of stitches across and down (see Adapting Projects, pages 130–131) and draw this shape onto graph paper (remember, one square = one stitch).

It may be necessary at this stage to be a little flexible about the size, in order to accommodate a patterned border; for example, if you allow for an extra stitch or two in either or both directions, the pattern may work out neater at the corners.

Most patterns are built up from smaller ones and repeated as required. The pattern shape can be reversed and added to until you have formed a pleasing design. Let your imagination have a free hand and play around with a patchwork shape, perhaps an octagon, square or triangle. Often, the simplest shapes can make the most attractive patterns. Remember, before starting to embroider you must be happy with what you have drawn. Does the balance of pattern look right for the finished size? Is there too much or too little border pattern? Is the design so fussy that it will be extremely difficult to work? Can you reduce the number of colours and still get the look you want? It is worth taking as much time as necessary to get the pattern right on graph paper, as it is a lot easier to erase a pencil mark than to undo miniature embroidery! Fundamentally, if you like the look on graph paper, you should be happy with the finished result.

Designing a border

Having designed the main part of your pattern, it is time to think about a border. This can be just one or several rows of tent stitch, or a more ambitious border using a patchwork shape. Start from the central line of

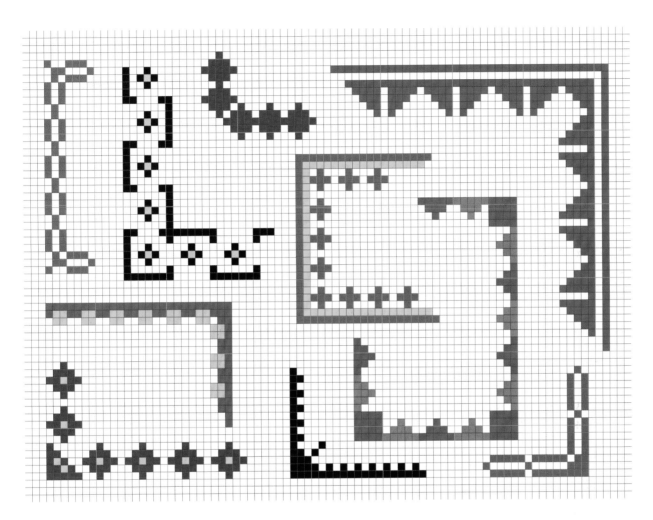

Examples of corner patterns

your design, along the top edge, drawing your chosen shape in both directions until you reach the corners. Do the same along the bottom edge, again starting from the centre and working outwards. Now start on the middle line of one side of your design and draw the same shape in both directions until you reach the corners. Do the same on the opposite side. You may be extremely lucky and find the pattern meets perfectly at the corners but, more likely, it won't. In this case, decide whether by taking the border in or out one or

two rows (nearer or further away from your central pattern) you will have the correct number of squares to make the pattern work. If not, treat the corner sections differently by creating an alternative pattern shape that works for all corners (see the chart above for a few suggestions).

So, do have a go. At the very worst you will have wasted a little time and paper but, at best, you will be well on the way to creating unique miniature embroidered items for your dolls' house.

Chapter 11

Golden Rules

Use only enough strands of thread in your needle to cover the fabric. The finished work should be delicate, not bulky.

Miniature embroidery can be tiring on the eyes, so try not to do too much at a time. I usually work for an hour or so, then get up and have a walk around – I might even pick up a duster!

If you see your embroidery thread beginning to kink as you are sewing, let your needle drop so that it untwists. This will give a smoother look to the way the stitches lie.

If you are not covering all the fabric with embroidery, i.e. in the case of three of the wall hangings, take extra care not to trail threads across the back of the fabric between one part of the pattern and another, as they will show. Instead, finish off under the colour you have just been working, cut the thread and start again in the new position.

Don't hold your needle too tightly: stitches are more likely to be pulled too tight if you are tense so that the thread will not cover the fabric as well and the fabric will become distorted.

In miniature embroidery, colours that are too similar simply blend into one another, making it difficult to see the pattern. If you are choosing your own colours, make sure that the difference in each of them is distinct enough to be seen. If you are unsure, work a few small sample pieces.

Try to keep the embroidery clean. It helps to have it covered when you are not working on it. Although most embroidery threads are colourfast, I try to avoid the need to wash the finished item.

Do not neglect the appearance of the back of your work. Invariably, people interested in the piece will turn it over to see how neat it is. Try to start and finish each colour under the stitches already worked in that colour. (For more details see Starting and finishing your thread, page 19.)

Position unwanted threads at the front of your work to be picked up again as needed. It helps to have several needles in use at the same time, to avoid having to constantly re-thread your needle.

Lastly, never be afraid to experiment. Miniature embroidery is very economical, as such small amounts of fabric and thread are used. So, if you don't like what you have done, just start again. I never throw away my mistakes but keep them in plastic sleeves, in a folder, for future reference.

Thread Conversion Chart

This conversion chart is for guidance only, as exact comparisons are not always possible.

Anchor	DMC	Madeira	Anchor	DMC	Madeira	Anchor	DMC	Madeira	Anchor	DMC	Madeira
1	blanc	2401	149	336	1006	303	742	114	843	3012	1606
6	353	2605	150	823	1007	305	743	109	846	936	1507
8	3824	304	152	939	1009	306	725	2514	847	928	1805
10	351	406	160	813	1105	307	783	2514	850	926	1707
13	347	211	161	826	1012	309	781	2213	856	370	1509
19	817	407	162	825	1107	311	977	2301	858	524	1512
20	3777	2502	164	824	2505	314	741	203	871	3041	806
22	815	2501	185	964	1112	316	740	202	876	503	1703
35	3705	411	186	959	1113	323	722	307	877	502	1205
38	3731	611	188	943	2706	326	720	309	878	501	1205
45	814	2606	189	991	2705	330	947	205	879	500	1204
46	6566	210	205	912	1213	332	946	207	885	739	2014
47	304	510	206	564	1210	333	608	206	887	3046	2206
49	3689	607	214	368	2604	334	606	209	888	3045	2112
50	605	613	215	320	1310	335	606	209	889	610	2105
52	957	2707	216	367	1310	337	922	403	894	3326	813
54	956	611	217	319	1312	341	355	314	895	223	812
68	3687	604	227	701	1305	343	932	1710	896	315	810
69	3685	2609	236	3799	1713	349	301	2306	897	221	2606
70	*	2608	241	703	1307	351	400	2304	899	3022	1906
74	3354	606	245	701	1305	352	300	2304	903	3032	2002
75	3733	505	246	986	1404	357	975	2602	905	3021	1904
76	961	505	253	772	1604	358	801	2008	968	778	808
78	600	2609	254	3348	1409	359	898	2007	969	816	809
85	3609	710	255	907	1410	360	938	2005	970	3726	2609
94	917	706	256	906	1411	368	436	2011	1012	948	305
97	554	711	264	3348	1409	369	435	2010	1014	355	2502
99	552	2714	265	471	1308	371	433	2602	1021	963	404
101	550	713	266	470	1502	372	738	2013	1023	760	405
102	*	2709	267	469	1503	376	842	1910	1024	3328	406
108	210	2711	268	937	1504	378	841	2601	1025	347	407
109	209	2711	269	895	1507	379	840	2601	1027	223	812
112	*	2710	276	3770	2314	380	838	2005	1036	336	1712
117	341	901	278	472	1414	382	3371	2004	1037	3756	2504
118	340	902	279	734	1610	386	746	2512	1042	369	1701
122	3807	2702	280	581	1611	390	822	1908	1070	993	
127	823	1008	289	307	103	397	3204	1901	1072	993	
137	798	911	292	3078	102	398	415	1802	1074	3814	
139	797	912	293	727	110	400	317	1714	1089	996	
140	3755	910	295	726	109	403	310	2400	1090	996	
145	799	910	297	973	105	683	890	1705	5975	356	401
146	798	911	298	972	107	781			1335		
147	797	912	300	677	111	842	3013	1605	1345		

Mail Order Worldwide Suppliers

SIESTA
Unit D, Longmeadow Industrial Estate, Three Legged Cross
Wimborne, Dorset BH21 6RD England
Tel/fax: +44 (0)1202 813363
www.siestaframes.com

(Suppliers of frames, scissors, magnifying lamps, etc.)

WILLOW FABRICS
95, Town Lane, Mobberley, Knutsford, Cheshire
WA16 7HH England
Tel: +44 (0)1565 872225   Fax: +44 (0)1565 872239
Email: major@willowfabrics.com   www.willowfabrics.com

(Suppliers of evenweave fabrics, threads, needles, scissors and sundry items.)

About the Author

Margaret Major has practised embroidery for many years, and having a keen interest in dolls' houses decided to take up miniature embroidery. In 2001 Margaret gained a qualification in miniature embroidery and has subsequently taught the craft from her home in a small, picturesque village in the south-east of England. In addition to her teaching, Margaret exhibits her work at dolls' house fairs and regularly designs and markets her own kits.

Index

Index

Index

UPHOLSTERY

TOYMAKING

DOLLS' HOUSES AND MINIATURES

Crafts

MAGAZINES
WOODTURNING ◆ WOODCARVING
◆ FURNITURE & CABINETMAKING
THE ROUTER ◆ NEW
WOODWORKING ◆ THE DOLLS'
HOUSE MAGAZINE
OUTDOOR PHOTOGRAPHY ◆
BLACK & WHITE PHOTOGRAPHY
TRAVEL PHOTOGRAPHY ◆
MACHINE KNITTING NEWS
KNITTING ◆ GUILD OF MASTER
CRAFTSMEN NEWS

The above represents a full list of all titles currently
published or scheduled to be published.
All are available direct from the Publishers or through
bookshops, newsagents and specialist retailers.
To place an order, or to obtain a complete catalogue, contact:

**GMC Publications,
Castle Place, 166 High Street, Lewes,
East Sussex BN7 1XU United Kingdom
Tel: 01273 488005 Fax: 01273 402866
E-mail: pubs@thegmcgroup.com**

Orders by credit card are accepted